PROPHETIC
SNIPERS
VOLUME 1

A REVELATORY GUIDE TO PROPHETIC
ACCURACY IN PRAYER

TERI M. JONES

PROPHETIC SNIPERS products are also available at special quantity discounts for bulk purchase sales promotions, premiums, fund-raising, and educational purposes.

For details, write to propheticsnipersintl@gmail.com or call 470-236-3131.

PROPHETIC SNIPERS, Volume 1 by Teri M. Jones under Teri Jones Ministries is a self-published manuscript, in Atlanta, Georgia.

Unless otherwise noted, all Scripture quotations are from the Holy Bible, King James version.

Cover Art by: Embyrd Designs, www.embyrddesigns.com
Strategy for editing and project management by: KeenerKoncepts, LLC, www.keenerkoncepts.com

Visit the author's website at www.terijonesministries.com.

ISBN-10: 1979744777
ISBN-13: 978-1979744775

Printed in the United States of America

ACKNOWLEDGEMENTS

To my Lord and Savior Jesus Christ, whom I have loved for over 20 years. *Lord, I love you more today than I did yesterday.*

I acknowledge the best husband on earth! Thank you, my darling for always supporting and pushing me to be better. Thank you for your constructive criticism. It made me push to the finish. I love you with all of me!

I acknowledge my mom, who is one of my biggest supporters! I love you dearly. Thank you for birthing me.

I acknowledge my leaders, Apostle Travis Jennings and Pastor Stephanie Jennings. You have seen me grow into who I am today. Thank you for believing, trusting and investing in me. The reward will be great!

I acknowledge KeenerKoncepts, LLC for helping me organize and perfect this manual and website. Thank you for working so diligently.

I acknowledge Minister Eric Byrd for the artwork of this project.

Lastly, (but not least), I acknowledge all of the prayer warriors who will read this manual. Your life will never be the same.

I DECLARE that after reading this manual, you will shift into a new mantle of a Prophetic Sniper!

FOREWORD

~

I met Teri years before I knew I would lead a ministry of gifted, anointed and talented spiritual sons and daughters, whom God would entrust me to train, develop and deploy. We both worked at a secular company in the Atlanta area and I was serving as an elder at my local church. Actually, she knew my wife (my fiancé at the time) first, who was also working at the same company. Even back then, I can remember Teri's love for God's people, her consistency in salvation, her fervency for the Lord, her influence and her love for prayer and intercession. I remain amazed to know that our time there at that company, in that particular secular atmosphere, was a "prophetic capture" in preparation of how God would later align us all together for the purpose of ministry.

I can also recall times of personal ministry with Teri right there in the break room, during our lunch hour. We would all spend so much time discussing the word and she would ask me questions and I would begin to minister to her – or in other words, we had church right there in that lunchroom! I had no idea that I would go on to pastor Teri as her spiritual father or that she would even become such a vital asset and partner to our ministry as she has been so faithfully.

Fast forward a few years later, I'm now in full-time ministry, Stephanie and I are now married with a young family and we've just launched our new ministry, the Harvest Tabernacle church. One particular day, we're at the local mall, enjoying family time and destiny intervenes yet again. We see an old familiar face and "bump" into Teri. We exchanged greetings and hugs and we chatted for a bit. Though she had matured, I could see that the same fire for the Lord she had when I met her, was still there. I could see that the passion and fervency she had for kingdom and for the people of God was still burning brightly. I could see that the seeds planted years ago through our meeting and in that break room had taken root. Little did any of us know meeting on this day was a destiny-ordained and kingdom-designed encounter facilitated by God.

It felt like old times again but we were all more mature – naturally and spiritually. Teri was now intercessory leader of a prayer ministry at the local church where she was serving at the time and Stephanie and I were new leaders with a young church and a young family. During this conversation, I now sensed a strong purpose with Teri that went well beyond just an evangelical break time in the company's lunchroom. She had an intense hunger for her purpose in the Kingdom of God and her destiny. She carried an undeniable burden to see people's lives transformed, to see them set free and walking in God's purpose for their lives. At that moment, I sensed a shift in the prophetic dynamic in our relationship that was about to occur. Somehow we knew that extending her an invitation to visit our church was destiny and it would be life changing for her and for us.

Teri visited once and she kept visiting...and kept visiting...and kept visiting. She even brought other visitors and one of those visitors was her mother who ended up partnering with our ministry well before Teri did! One hot, summer day in June of 2005, after a powerful move of God, Teri *finally* decided to partner with our ministry. We were much smaller ministry back then so it didn't take long for Teri to integrate within our ministry family.

After spending much time with Teri and observing her faithfulness and commitment to The Harvest Tabernacle vision, I appointed her to lead our intercessory team. It has been such an honor to see her commitment, growth and development to the things of God. She has matriculated under our covering from sister, to minister and to then to Elder. All while leading our ministry's intercessory efforts and training other intercessors. In 2013, through much prayer, we proudly consecrated her as one of the pastors of our great church.

Teri has never sought out a platform. She has never sought praise or adoration and she has always placed the agenda of God as top priority one – a characteristic of a *true* intercessor. Teri's fulfillment comes from God's delight. She is a kingdom intercessor and as one who "shamars" (watches, protects and covers). She has been validated as a governmental prophet.

We are so very proud of Teri's new project. We are proud to call her a daughter of the Harvest Tabernacle Church. I am ecstatic in the way that God continues to stretch her and how her hunger for next level ministry never ceases. This manuscript has been a long time coming and she has packed over 20 years worth of intercessory wisdom and experience for kingdom. I've witnessed and helped cultivate her growth and I know that the information and strategies concerning prayer and intercession for the Body of Christ and for this hour is *desperately needed.* **It's no longer church as usual so it can't be prayer as usual!**

--DR. TRAVIS JENNINGS

Senior Pastor, The Harvest Tabernacle Church, Atlanta, Georgia

Author of: *The Gathering of Champions, Life on Turbo, Lifeguard* and *Faith for the Gold.*

CONTENTS

INTRODUCTION

What are Prophetic Snipers?

Be Sober, be vigilant, because your adversary the devil, as a roaring lion, walketh about, seeking whom he may devour; Whom resist steadfast in the faith, knowing that the same afflictions are accomplished in your brethren that are in the world; But the God of all grace, who hath called us unto his eternal glory by Christ Jesus, after that ye have suffered awhile, make you perfect, stablish, strengthen, settle you. − **1 Peter 5: 8-10 (KJV)**

Be well balanced (temperate, sober of mind), be vigilant and cautious at All times; for that enemy of yours the devil, roams around like a lion roaring(in fierce hunger), seeking someone to seize (To lay hold of or take possession of by force) upon and devour. − **1 Peter 5:8 (AMP)**

~

We are now living in a time where the people of God have become ignorant of the devil's devices. This current state is primarily due to a lack of prayer and a lack of personal connection to God. Most would say that the god of this world has blinded the minds. However, this statement does not pertain to believers only, but it also refers to those who do not believe. This fact is presented in **2 Corinthians 4:4**, which states: **in whom the god of this world hath blinded the minds of them which believe not, lest the light of the glorious gospel of Christ, who is the image of God, should shine unto them.**

God especially does <u>not</u> want believers to be ignorant of the devil's devices and this is why prayer is crucial to him and so

1

beneficial for believers. **1 Thessalonians 5:17** encourages us to pray without ceasing. God admonishes us to stay in the posture of prayer because our enemy never sleeps. Not that our focus should be constantly on our enemy, but as believers, we must now have relevant understanding about the enemy's tactics for more effective prayer. Not only does prayer keep us in a place of God's presence and in a position of hearing his voice, but it is this posture that God releases heavenly intelligence and strategies for life. It is this connection that allows us to be knowledgeable of every trick, booby trap, tactic and move of the enemy. At times, it is merely distractions or laziness that keeps the Body of Christ in "sleep mode" at a time when we should be the most vigilant.

> And that knowing the time, that now it is high time to awake out of sleep; for now is our salvation nearer than when we believed. **Romans 13:11**

You might ask – what exactly is a sniper? A sniper is a marksman who shoots at an exposed enemy from a concealed (a place out of sight) position. Snipers typically have specialized training and use distinct high-precision rifles. At times, prophetic snipers may experience hands-on warfare training, directly from the enemy. Snipers are often on the front lines and are in dangerous areas of the highest military activity. They have to be tactical at all times; often acting on intelligence they have studied for long amounts of time about their enemy. A sniper's ultimate objective on any assignment is to **take out their enemy**. For a kingdom prophetic sniper, **2 Corinthians 10:4** states: **For the weapons of our warfare are not carnal, but mighty through God to the pulling down of strongholds**. Therefore, a spiritual sniper uses a heavenly arsenal and thereby must be trained and must become skilled in the art of warfare.

The term sniper was first attested in 1824, incorporated with word "sharpshooter". The actual verb "to snipe" originated in the 1770's among soldiers in British India where a hunter skilled enough to kill an elusive enemy was dubbed a "sniper".

In modern warfare, another primary function of the sniper is to provide detailed survey of an enemy's territory from a concealed position and if necessary, to reduce the enemy's fighting ability by taking out high value targets (especially officers, communication and other personnel). Military snipers are also trained in camouflage and field craft. Spiritually speaking, *prophetic snipers* are those who fight high-ranking demons. **Ephesians 6:10-12** states: **Finally my brethren, be strong in the Lord and the power of his might; put on the whole armor of God, that ye may be able to stand against the wiles of the devil; For we wrestle not against flesh and blood, but against principalities, against powers, against the rulers of the darkness of this world, against spiritual wickedness in high places.**

The sniper also incorporates a strategy called *psychological warfare*. This includes the use of non-physical techniques to mislead, intimidate, demoralize, or otherwise influence the thinking or behavior of an opponent. The purpose: to wear down the enemy with frustration and to distract.

It's now time for real warriors to arise and take their rightful place of authority. It's time for real warriors to be fervent in spirit while serving the Lord. There is an urgency in the Body of Christ to awake! The enemy is seeking to snuff out the believer, demolish mandates and destroy destinies. He is studying kingdom. He is **watching world-changers and he is preparing to make his move. But God has a counter-attack!** He's raising up a new type of intercessor and releasing an anointing for called-out, committed and consecrated **Prophetic Snipers!**

CHAPTER 1

THE JOURNEY OF AN INTERCESSOR

~

By definition, an intercessor is a person, who by calling or by nature, chooses to be a mediator (a go-between) on behalf of those who cannot, will not or are unable to pray for themselves. Intercessors make requests, urge, plead, beg, counsel, discuss, risk, sacrifice, intervene, disrupt, stand in place of and make war regarding issues to God (or on behalf of God) for an individual(s), home, a church, a region, a city, the state, the nation and even concerning global matters. Intercessors may also mediate between the enemy on behalf of these very same groups.

There is a difference between a person who is called to be an intercessor and a person who prays. Anyone can pray and the bible states in **1 Thessalonians 5:17** that we must **pray without ceasing**. **Luke 21:36** states and **watch ye therefore, and pray always**. However, an important distinction to be aware of is that everyone who prays are not necessarily intercessors. Intercessors walk with the favor of God to impact and change God's heart on specific, intimate and general matters presented in prayer.

Intercessors are called, but few are chosen. To be chosen is to have gone through fire and to have yielded to God's sovereignty through death to self. This process also includes yielding to God to perfect the character and alignment of one's body, soul and spirit to his image. **It is surely a death process.**

An intercessor may walk their whole life in preparation for one moment in history – and that moment is the one moment they cast their vote and pray one prayer. It is like Moses when he interceded for Israel. To be clear, intercessors are not simply prayer warriors who pray all the time and thus the quantity of their prayers is what bears weight in the kingdom; rather it is their sacrificial and unselfish walk with the Lord. It is their total submission to the service and the call of the Lord that bears weight in the kingdom!

<u>**The Beginnings of an Intercessor**</u>

There are several key ingredients that helps in identifying a true kingdom intercessor and the characteristics to consider when developing an intercessory gift:

1. **Desire**

   Psalms 37:4 states, **Delight thyself also in the Lord; and he shall give thee the desires of thine heart.**

   Psalms 27:4 also declares, **One thing have I desire of the Lord, that will I seek after; that I may dwell in the house of the Lord all the days of my life, to behold the beauty of the Lord, and to enquire in his temple.**

God wants us to desire what he desires and hate what he hates. He gives you the desire to execute his will.

I can remember one afternoon while at home cleaning (this was before I knew I was called to be an intercessor), I was praying and worshipping the Lord and suddenly I begin to say, "Lord, I want to pray for people! I really have a desire to pray for people!" I didn't know why I was saying this aloud but I recall this thought being so heavy on my heart. My roommate was actually reading a book on intercession at the time. I begin to search intently for the very same book I saw her reading. I wanted to know more about intercession and this thought that suddenly invaded my worship time. After I purchased the book, I read the entire book in two days! The information was feeding a divine desire that was placed directly in my heart about prayer and intercession. It was at that very moment God begin to give me another revelation on the scripture, "he will *give* you the desires of your heart". God, I can honestly say, put that desire in my heart. I knew that it was his desire that I would pray and intercede on behalf of his people. This new desire in me grew deeply and I could not shake it. In that season of my life, God begin to give me more revelation about the mantle of intercession. I started to embrace what he was calling me to do in the kingdom wholeheartedly. As I grew in God, the gift in me grew - just as Jesus grew and waxed strong in the spirit; **Luke 1:80 and the child grew, and waxed strong in spirit, and was in the deserts till the day of his shewing unto Israel.**

2. Passion

Hebrews 4:14-15 KJV, Seeing then that we have a great high priest, that is passed into the heavens, Jesus the son of God, let us hold fast our profession. For we have not an high priest which cannot be touched with the feelings of our infirmities; but was in all points tempted like as we are, yet without sin.

Hebrews 4:14-15 MSG, Now that we know what we have-Jesus, this great High priest with ready access to God- let's not let it slip through our fingers; we don't have a priest who is out of touch with our reality. He's been through weakness and testing, experienced it all-all but the sin.

Once you have made a conscious decision to fully embrace your call as an intercessor, an immediate passion should develop within you for God's people and his church. I heard a great man of God declare: "if you pray for someone for 30 days you will develop love and passion for whom you are praying for". The more you begin to pray on behalf of another, the more it makes you spiritually concerned for them and for others. This process enables you to walk in a greater level of compassion for the body of Christ overall. **Let this mind be in you that was also in Christ Jesus.**

> And there came a leper to him, beseeching him, and kneeling down to him, and saying unto him, If thou wilt, thou canst make me clean. V 41; And Jesus, moved with compassion, put forth his hand, and touched him, and saith unto him, I will; be thou clean. **Mark 1:40-41**

3. Willingness

The strength and energy required to completely execute and endure the many assignments of intercession that comes divinely and directly from God.

Phil 2:13 KJV, For it is God which worketh in you both to will and to do of his good pleasure.

Phil 2:13 MSG, That energy is God's energy, an energy deep within you, God himself willing and working at what will give him the most pleasure.

It is a guarantee that an intercessor's flesh will tire and become weak at some point on their journey, but the more an intercessor learns to die to their will, God's will shall come forth. When Jesus became weak on his way to the cross (his ultimate assignment here on earth), his flesh fought so hard with the will of God to obey that he began to sweat "great drops of blood".

Luke 22:42 KJV, Father, if thou be willing, remove this cup from me; nevertheless not my will, but thine, be done.

Luke 22:42 MSG, Father, remove this cup from me. But please, not what I want. What do you want?

The place of Gethsemane is the place in an intercessor's walk with God where they must command their flesh to DIE! The intercessor's journey will intersect with Gethsemane at multiple times on their journey and they must learn to **press** in order to execute the will of God.

The Language of an Intercessor

The dictionary's definition of *language* is the method of human communication, either spoken or written, consisting on the use of words in a structured and conventional way. Another description of language is the system of communication used by a particular community or country. Here's my favorite explanation of "language" which is the development, acquisition, maintenance and use of complex systems of communication particularly the human ability to do so; and a language is any specific example of such a system. In other words, we can surmise that language is key to our very existence and so is the prophetic language of an intercessor's world.

Here are a few major ingredients intercessors must integrate within their language.

1. Spiritual Discernment

A true intercessor usually has a gift of discerning of spirits. It is important for them to know, through the Holy Spirit, what is of God and what is not of God. **1 Corinthians 12:10, to another the working of miracles, to another prophecy; to another**

discerning of spirits.

The gift of discernment, as it relates to the language of the intercessor, may also translate into having the ability to discern atmospheres. Discernment also includes sensing the activities of demonic influences that may hinder a move of God for a particular moment. Make no mistake about it, the gift of discernment is not for an individual to think they are better than another, but the discerning of spirits is for the purpose of lifting up a standard for God so that he can be glorified.

1. Prophetic Insight

There is discernment and then there is insight. Intercessors should have prophetic insight about the spirit realm concerning not only what is good and what is evil, but intercessors should also have an understanding of what is happening or what is about to happen and why. **Insight is the capacity to gain an accurate and deep, intuitive understanding of a person or thing.** How much insight an intercessor receives is based on an intercessor's *function, assignment, level and maturity*.

> Son of Man, speak to the Children of thy people, and say unto them, when I bring the sword upon a land, if the people of the land take a man of their coasts, and set him for their watchman; If when he seeth the sword come upon the land, he blow the trumpet, and warn the people. **Ezekiel 33: 2-3**

Though an intercessor may have insight about demonic activity, there should also be a balance – meaning, intercessors should have insight of what is good, what is in order, what is on God's heart and mind, and what is in his will. In other words, a balanced intercessor should also have an awareness and discernment of heavenly activity.

> And Elisha prayed, and said, Lord, I pray thee, open his
> eyes, that he may see. And the Lord opened the eyes of the
> young man; and he saw: and, behold, the mountain was full
> of horses and chariots of fire round about Elisha. **2 Kings
> 6:17**

3. Relentless Prayer

Intercessors should have a praying, oppressively constant, and incessant spirit at *all* times. A true intercessor is ready at the drop of a dime. They must always have an open spirit and an open heart; prepared for the Father to download his will. **However, intercession is not always convenient for the intercessor.** Intercessors must receive the Father's download and be prepared to pray, release, declare, decree, or execute his will in the earth − as it is in heaven. True intercessors **ultimately** belong to God.

> But it came to pass, that when Sanballat, and Tobiah, and
> the Arabians, and the Ammonites, and the Ashdodites, heard
> that the walls of Jerusalem were made up, and that the
> breaches began to be stopped, then they were very wroth,
> And conspired all of them together to come and to fight
> against Jerusalem, and to hinder it, Nevertheless we made
> our prayer unto our God, and set a watch against them day
> and night, because of them. **Nehemiah 4:7-9**

> Be sober, be vigilant; because your adversary the devil, as a
> roaring lion, walketh about, seeking whom he may devour.
> **1 Peter 5: 8**

What makes and defines a Prophetic Intercessor?

There is a season on this journey of becoming an effective, kingdom intercessor that God will allow a time of *training, testing* and *triumphing* in order to allow the development of the gift of intercession to develop. Military soldiers often endure a time of training in order to introduce them to the type of duress they may undergo in the field. They spend months in basic training and then based on their skillset, often endure more time of training within their particular field of expertise. However, *true* soldiers do not actually become soldiers until they are on the battlefield.

> My brethren, count it all joy when ye fall into divers temptations, knowing this, that the trying of your faith worketh patience, but let patience have her perfect work, that ye may be perfect and entire, wanting nothing. **James 1:2-4**

Training

Intercessors must go through a season of one-on-one training with God. At each level of growth, God will require a time where he trains the intercessor divinely. This training goes from faith to faith and glory to glory. **2 Corinthians 3:18** states, **But we all, with open face beholding as in a glass the glory of the Lord, are changed into the same image from glory to glory, even as by the spirit of the Lord.** I will go more in detail concerning this topic in the subsequent chapters.

Testing

Every intercessor must be proven through a series of wilderness experiences in three areas: 1) the lust of the eye, 2) lust of the flesh, and 3) the pride of life. God has to know he can trust the intercessor. They must pass each test and with each success comes another level of glory.

Triumphing

Lastly, intercessors must engage in multiple levels and with multiple rankings of demonic warfare in order to obtain the power to pull down their particular level of influence and wickedness. Every intercessor must understand that there is always an ongoing war in the spirit between truth and perversion, good and evil, light and darkness, and God's will and Satan's will. Just as heaven has a ranking order of angels, hell also has a ranking order of demons.

Against popular belief, a person cannot just wake up out of their sleep and arbitrarily say they are fighting principalities, powers, ruler spirits. Now, God has given us power to tread over the enemy (**Luke 10:19**), but there is a maturity an intercessor must grow and develop into in order to contend with these levels of demons AND obtain victory. Just as there are special operation teams in the military, **there is also an anointing specific to this type of warfare.**

The Warfare of the Intercessor

There will be a time in an intercessor's journey where they will encounter the type of warfare that will attempt to make the intercessor give up on the assignment God has called them to complete. All intercessors must cross this road on multiple occasions in their lives. It can also be an effective strategy of the enemy which is to distract, derail and ultimately destroy the assignment and agenda of God.

1. Attempted backlash of the enemy

Most of the time, the enemy will send an attack against an intercessor when they have witnessed breakthrough(s) in an area where they have targeted their prayers. **In 2 Kings 18**, as soon as Elijah obtained victory over the false prophets on Mount Moriah, Jezebel sent an attack to chase off Elijah in an effort to cause him to give up. Elijah's effectiveness made him a target. **This will happen.**

2. Accusations of the enemy

The enemy will also attempt to discourage true intercessors

through a series of accusations – both inwardly and outwardly. Inward accusations may be accessible by the enemy through a broken soul. A broken soul occurs when there is unhealed hurts, scars and disappointment as a result of trauma (rape, molestation, abuse, rejection, abandonment and etc.). A broken soul is a wide-open door which gives the enemy legal access and may allow inward accusation from the enemy in the form of harassing thoughts about your past, attacks on your self-esteem and identity; which could prevent you from walking fully in your authority.

Outward accusations from the enemy comes in the form of "the accuser of the brethren". The enemy will attempt to use other people to form lies about your identity, your character, your cause and your motives. His goal: to discredit and nullify an intercessor's authority and influence. He wants to limit or hinder an intercessor's ability to tear down his kingdom. He seeks to silence the intercessors. **Accusations WILL HAPPEN! However, the victory is in knowing that the accuser is already defeated!**

> And I heard a loud voice saying in heaven, Now is come salvation, and strength, and the kingdom of our God, and the power of his Christ: for the accuser of our brethren is cast down, which accused them before our God day and night.[11] And they overcame him by the blood of the Lamb, and by the word of their testimony; and they loved not their lives unto the death. **Revelation 12:10-11 KJV**

3. Aim of the enemy

If an intercessor is effective in their assignment(s), then the enemy will focus and concentrate his efforts on removing an intercessor from their post(s). The enemy will attempt to distract and destroy the prophets and intercessors of the house of God. This is why intercessors must have a sound strategy and a stable spiritual life to counteract, confront and combat the tactics of the enemy.

There must be *continuous* covering of the intercessor through God's covering, his word, and their leader.

An intercessor must ensure they are under good, prophetic leadership that understands and honor the gift, anointing and assignment(s) on an intercessor's life.

PROPHETIC ACTIVATION:

Lord, thank you for the journey I am about to embark upon! Thank you that you have placed a hunger and a thirst within me to go to the next level of prayer. I thank you now for next level intercession impartation. I command my spirit man to comprehend and receive. I recognize that you are calling me higher in prayer and intercession for such a time as this. Thank you for your faithfulness.

In Jesus' Name. Amen!

CHAPTER 2

THE STRATEGY OF AN INTERCESSOR

Simon, "stay on your toes", Satan has tried his best to separate all of you from me, like chaff from wheat, but Jesus declared to Simon, I have prayed for you in particular that you not give in or give out. – **Luke 22: 31-32 (MSG)**

~

End-time intercessors must now incorporate strategies to contend with the enemy in this hour, just as Jesus told Peter in **Luke 22:31-32.** Jesus admonished Peter to, "stay on your toes" and when you have endured a time of testing, turn to your companions and encourage them through their time of testing. An intercessor will go through seasons of testing for purging and purification. After an intercessor has passed every level of test, then an intercessor will obtain the power, endurance, and weight that is necessary to help others endure. Intercession is a primary vehicle for helping fellow brothers and sisters in Christ bear trying seasons of their lives.

Strategy is the science and art of military command exercised to contend with an enemy in combat under advantageous conditions. It is a carefully planned out method. It is the art of devising or employing plans or strategies toward an intended goal. A strategy is an *arrangement, blueprint, master plan or system*. It is an end-time tool needed in your spiritual arsenal in order to execute a heavenly assignment or agenda and to carry a particular mantle.

> For though we walk in the flesh, we do not war after the flesh. For the weapons of our warfare are not carnal, but mighty through God to the pulling down of strongholds, casting down imaginations and every high thing that exalteth itself against the knowledge of God and bringing into captivity every thought to the obedience of Christ; and having in a readiness to revenge all disobedience, when your obedience is fulfilled. **2 Corinthians 10:3-6**

For this purpose and for this age, an intercessor **must have a strategic plan** before embarking on their journey so they can effectively advance to their next level of intercession. Here are a few key tactics a developing intercessor must incorporate into their strategy:

Commitment

To put into charge or trust (entrust); to pledge or assign to some particular course or use. This is an intercessor's strength – the grace from God to be committed to an assignment of prayer that God has assigned to them in order to bring it to completion.

> But unto every one of us is given grace according to the measure of the gift of Christ. **Ephesians 4:7**

Passion

A strong feeling; love; an object or person of affection or enthusiasm.

> Finally, be ye all of one mind, having compassion one of another, love as brethren, be pitiful, be courteous. **1 Peter 3:8**

> But whoso hath this world's good, and seeth his brother have need, and shutteth up his bowels of compassion from him, how dwelleth the love of God in him? V18-my little children, let us not love in word, neither in tongue; but in deed and in truth. **I John 3:17**

> If you see some brother or sister in need and have the means to do something about it but turn a cold shoulder and do nothing, what happens to God's love? It disappears, and you made it disappear. **1 John 3:17 MSG**

As we see in scripture, it is not hard for an intercessor to see a need in someone's life, in a church or an event and them not be moved with compassion to stand in the gap. In many scriptures, Jesus stated that he was moved with compassion whenever it related to God's will for people, for breakthroughs and deliverance.

Urgency

Urgency is the calling for immediate attention (pressing). Every intercessor should have a sense of urgency when it comes to prayer or their prayer assignment. There should be something burning in an intercessor's spirit when there is a high need of a request from heaven. We should be quick to move on the word of the Lord whether he speaks a logos or rhema word. Your heart should cry: "There is a need!!"

> And they said one to another, did not out heart burn within us, while he talked with us by the way, and while he opened to us the scriptures? **Luke 24: 32**

Who are Prophetic Intercessors?

Prophetic intercessors are individuals who have the ability to receive an immediate prayer request from God and pray about it in a divinely anointed utterance. When an intercessor can see the enemy and his attacks a mile away or see God preparing to move on behalf of his people or any situation before it manifests. Prophetic intercessors are able to counteract the enemy. Likewise, when a prophetic intercessor sees God getting ready to move, they have the ability to help birth God's move forth. In other words, prophetic intercessors have intimate access to the Throne Room of God to pray his will on earth. Prophetic intercessors are given prophetic insight of a matter before it manifests in the earth. This type of access **does not** give prophetic intercessors the right to walk in pride or arrogance, but it is a humbling yet powerful way to serve the King. Throne room access requires another level of "yes" (surrender) in an intercessor's heart. Intercessors must always be available for God to use them as a vessel of honor. **I believe there are levels to this type of honor.**

> Nevertheless the foundation of God standeth sure, having this seal, the Lord knoweth them that are his and let everyone that nameth the name of Christ depart from iniquity; But in a great house there are not only vessels of gold and of silver, but also of wood and of earth; and some to honour, and some to dishonor; If a man therefore purge himself from these, he shall be a vessel unto honour, sanctified, and meet for the master's use and prepared unto every good work.
> **2 Timothy 2:19-21**

Here we see different levels of use for the kingdom. God *must* trust you at every level. In the Olympics, there are three levels of medals. There are bronze, silver and gold medals. If you notice, they always acknowledge the bronze winner first which is third place. The bronze medalist is also usually positioned on a podium that is lower than the other two medalists because there are levels.

God must trust an intercessor and will ensure they can pass each level of testing.

The Bronze Level Intercessor

At this level of intercession, an intercessor may experience contending with headache demons. Here an intercessor may also engage with vexing spirits from a co-worker. An intercessor will be tested through their family, foes and friends at this level of intercession. God is certifying that the intercessor can endure through pressures from family members, attacks on salvation and etc. At the bronze level, should God lay someone on the intercessor's heart to intercede for, will they obey? Or, if he wakes up an intercessor in the middle of the night to intercede, will they obey, get up and pray?

The Silver Level Intercessor

This level of intercession requires the intercessor's gift to be tested through envy, jealousy, competition, discord and the like. Here is when an intercessor's anointing has increased and the devil knows it! Therefore, he will use provocation in an attempt to cause the intercessor to react in the flesh when it should be understood that the activity is demonic and it is all spiritual – for we wrestle not against flesh and blood. It is at this level where an intercessor may contend with the hearts of wicked men and those who are open for the devil to use. Here, an intercessor may be fighting the evil thoughts, wicked imaginations, ill wishes and witchcraft attacks of others.

It is at this level where an intercessor will begin to engage witches and warlocks. Here is where the intercessor will have to walk in the fruit of the spirit; yet use their spiritual muscles and authority to counteract evil attacks. This level will sharpen an intercessor's spiritual senses. Here is where and intercessor will become keen in the spirit. The silver level is the onset of the intercessor's transition into **Prophetic Sniper** realm. The enemy knows that if an intercessor effectively walks this level out, the intercessor is well on their way to a higher rank in heaven and therefore a higher level of authority over the enemy's kingdom. **This is a warning!! The intercessor MUST NOT fail** this level by giving the enemy what he wants. The enemy wants the intercessor to give up plain and simple. The intercessor's endurance is stretching at this level and they *must* begin to draw closer to God and pull scriptures out of their belly to stand on.

> Looking unto Jesus the Author and Finisher of our faith; who for the joy that was set before him endured the cross, despising the shame, and is set down at the right hand of the throne of God. **Hebrews 12:2**

The Gold Level Intercessor

At this level, an intercessor is now walking in the power of **Ephesians 6:12, We wrestle not against flesh and blood, but against principalities, against powers, against the rulers of the darkness of this world, against spiritual wickedness in high places.** Here, an intercessor now begins to walk in a completely different level of intercession altogether.

An intercessor must walk through each of these demonic levels as outlined in Ephesians 6 to obtain true authority from Christ. As each level is obtained, an intercessor begins to walk in the type of power in Christ where these demonic powers and principalities are now disarmed. At this level, when an intercessor walks in a room the authority that they carry will cause higher-ranking demons to agitate, bow, leave or even dismantle altogether.

> And having spoiled principalities and powers, he made a shew of them openly, triumphing over them in it. **Col 2:15**

Characteristics of a True Intercessor

- **Love for people - 1 John 3:1, 1 John 4:7-21**

- **Knowledge of God's Word - 2 Timothy 2:15**

- **Willing to do the work - Philippians 2:13-14**

- **Fervency** - Must mean business

- **Awareness** - Sensitive to Holy Spirit and to the needs of others

- **Availability** - Must be available to God for his will) - **Romans 6:13**

- **Advocate** - One who goes in another's place to plead on their behalf, **Romans 8:26 and 1 Timothy 2:5**

- **Acceptance** - Must be able to pray for someone you dislike, **Matthew 5:44 and Romans 12:14**

- **Empathy** - Must be able to sense and feel the emotions and spiritual needs of others**, Hebrews 4:14-16**

- **Armor of God - Ephesians 6:10-18**

- **Authority - Luke 10:19 and Matthew 10:1**

- **Accountability** - To God to pray for those he lays on the intercessor's heart at a particular moment**, Jeremiah 17:9**

CHAPTER 3

WHO ARE YOU?
DISCOVERING YOUR ANOINTING

Then the word of the LORD came unto me saying, Before I formed thee in the belly I knew thee; and before thou camest forth out of the womb I sanctified thee, and I ordained thee a prophet unto the nations. Then said I, Ah, Lord GOD! behold, I cannot speak: for I am a child. But the LORD said unto me, Say not, I am a child: for thou shalt go to all that I shall send thee, and whatsoever I command thee thou shalt speak. Be not afraid of their faces: for I am with thee to deliver thee, saith the LORD. **- Jeremiah 1:4-8 KJV**

~

We are in a day where we not only need faith for our money, family, career and etc., but we also need faith to identify and embrace who we are in Christ. This is key in helping the intercessor effectively walk in the anointing as a prophetic sniper. Knowing who you are can help identify the enemy. For example: you may have more precision when identifying an enemy if you have the gift of discerning spirits. Or, you may have better accuracy when exposing the enemy if you have the gift of prophecy. If we are going to be effective in the kingdom, we must now have confidence in who we are and not in the world and its systems. We must conform to God's system by allowing our minds to align with the image and customs of Christ.

The enemy's job is to steal, kill and ultimately destroy who we were meant to be in the kingdom. Therefore, there will be a spirit of frustration that will attempt to attack the intercessor. This frustration comes from one's lack of knowledge regarding their identity and purpose. Frustration leads to fear and fear leads to failure. Because of the lack of assurance in identity, the Body of Christ may eventually covet or desire the callings, gifts and the purposes of others. God has declared in Jeremiah that he formed and knew us while we were in in our Mother's womb. **God has summoned (a call by authority to appear at a place to attend for duty) EACH of us to a particular assignment or task for the Glory of God.**

> Moreover whom he did predestinate, them he also called: and whom he called, them he also justified: and whom he justified, them he also glorified. What shall we then say to these things? If God be for us, who can be against us? He that spared not his own son, but delivered him up for us all, how shall he not with him also freely give us all things? Who shall lay anything to the charge of God's elect? It is God that justifies. This should eliminate all fears and cause us to walk in a boldness of who God created us to be. **Romans 8:30 KJV**

In the text of this chapter, **Jeremiah** served as the prophet to Judah. The purpose of this book was to urge God's people to turn from their sins and turn back to God. Jeremiah is a type of apostolic church of this day. His **audience** was Judah (the southern kingdom) and its capital city was Jerusalem. You must know the audience you are called to in order to discover the type of anointing on your life. Discovering and embracing this will eliminate a lot of REJECTION within. There may be a certain type of people you are called to initially, but once you accept your identity, you will begin to embrace this principle along your walk even more. Jeremiah was rejected by his neighbors (11:19-21), his family (12:6), the false priest and prophets (20:1-2; 28:1-17), friends (20:10), his audience (26:8) and the kings (36:23). Throughout his life Jeremiah stood alone, declaring God's message of doom. In the eyes of the world, Jeremiah was not a success, but in the eyes of God he was one of the most successful prophets in history. Success is measured by God which involves **obedience** and **faithfulness.** Regardless of the opposition and personal costs, Jeremiah boldly proclaimed the word of the Lord. We are in the end times and we must have boldness in order to fully walk in the anointing God has on our lives. When people don't except who we are (who God created us to be), one may become timid and draw back. There must be confidence in the fact that **He who began a good work in us will perform it until the day of Jesus Christ (Philippians 1:6)!** This assurance brings freedom and where the spirit of the Lord is there is liberty **(2 Corinthians 3:17).** When we try to be anyone else other than who and what God has made us, **this is bondage and counterfeit.**

There were four dynamics Jeremiah experienced:

God said,

1. I formed thee – This means he shaped and structured us as distinguished from its material. God has shaped us into his image. Another translation says the component of a thing that determines its kind. This means God will form you AND the anointing on your life to what HE has purposed for you to do.

> Now the God of peace, that brought again from the dead our Lord Jesus, that great shepherd of the sheep, through the blood of the everlasting covenant, make you perfect in every good work to do his will, working in you that which is well pleasing in his sight, through Jesus Christ to whom be glory forever. Amen. **Col 2:15**

2. I sanctified thee - He consecrated you, set you apart as hallowed for a special use. This revelation is discovered through a relationship with Christ. The more you seek after him to know the will of God for your life, the more he will sanctify you and use you for his glory.

> If a man therefore purge himself from these, he shall be a vessel unto honour, sanctified, and meet for the Master's use, and prepared unto every good work. **2 Timothy 2:21**

3. I ordained thee – He has officially invested and placed his authority in you. He has decreed a thing over your life and IT WILL be established.

> Thou shalt also decree a thing, and it shall be established unto thee; and the light shall shine upon thy ways. **Job 22:28**

Defining who you are in the Kingdom

Intercessors *must* operate under a senior leader. This means either an apostle, pastor, or a senior mentor in order to be developed. This starts by committing to and serving in a local church. Over the years, I have witnessed sons and daughters who want the "big payoff" of power and influence of their leader's anointing without going through the process – which begins with submission to a local church.

> Though thy beginning was small, yet thy latter end should greatly increase. **Job 8:7** KJV

We should not be anxious and want to skip the process of increasing; however, we should desire to move from faith to faith and from glory to glory. We must learn to be patient and graduate from one level of faith to another through serving in our local assemblies. Most people want to go to nations before they are ever developed under their leadership. An intercessor's leader will help add the necessary ingredients to a particular anointing. Intercessors must go through this development process in order to be effective.

Definition. The root word is define, which means providing clarity and expressing the essential nature of something. Development will give one the construct of what their purpose is defined for. Example: Why am I loud? Why am I particular? Why am I disturbed when things are out of order? As one grows and develops, they begin to understand why they were made the way they were. Everything begins to make sense and they understand that every thing has a purpose and that purpose is for God's glory.

> I will praise thee: for I am fearfully and wonderfully made: marvelous are thy works. **Psalms 139:14 KJV**
>
> I thank you, High God-your breathtaking!! Body and soul, I am marvelously made!! I worship in adoration-what a creation: You know me inside and out, you know every bone in my body: you know exactly how I was made, bit by bit, how I was sculpted from nothing into something. **Psalms 139:14-15 MSG**

Details. Implies knowing the intricacies; the extended treatment of or attention to a particular item.

> And the day following Paul went in with us unto James, and all the Elders were present; verse 19- and when he had saluted them, he declared particularly what things God had wrought among the gentiles by his ministry. **Acts 21:19-20**

Direction. Guidance or supervision of an action or conduct. For example: A son/daughter that needs apostolic direction from a spiritual father/mother or mentor. We can have the definition and detail, but if there is no apostolic direction and order, it may cancel everything else. The bible declares that we are like sheep that have gone astray. He has given us pastors to watch over our souls and he has given us a prophets to point us in the right direction.

Surely the Lord God will do nothing, but he revealed his secret unto his servants the Prophets. **Amos 3:7**

The fact is, God, the Master, does nothing without first telling his prophets the whole story. **Amos 3:7 MSG**

Knowing who you are through signs and patterns:

When you see a pattern in your life, this is often a sign of who you are. David had a pattern of a warrior. He fought and killed a lion, a bear, and an intruder of the sheep he was overseeing (**1 Sam 17**), before eventually killing the Philistine everyone was afraid of. Patterns are a snapshot of the history and even a small glimpse into the future of your life. **What are some of your life's patterns that are apparent to you?** You always get stuck with somebody's kids. People draw to you wherever you go. You always have the ability to bring resolution to problems in your family or work. You are always able to bring peace in any chaos. Every job you have worked, you seem to always end up ministering to someone in senior management.

I entered the workforce at the age of 14. My first job was McDonald's. I was so happy to get my first job. I was on this job for 1 year and they saw the leadership potential in me and promoted me to manager at the age of 15. From this job to every job since then, someone in management would see this gift of leadership and promote me to management in less then 6 months to a year. I've always attracted this type of favor from management. As I begin to understand the anointing on my life once I accepted Jesus Christ, God started to develop my intercession to pray for leaders. From leaders in government to leaders in churches, I walked in a prayer grace to cover and pray for leaders. Out of this developed the ability to teach others how to cover leaders, which we will discuss later.

Keys to knowing who you are as a person:

- Know your weaknesses
- Know your strengths
- Know your temperament
- Know your tolerance
- Know your kind (anointing, business etc.)
- Know the level of people you connect and relate with

Keys to knowing who you are in Christ:

- Know that you are a joint-heir with Christ
- Know that you are royalty (a royal priesthood)
- Know that POWER is in Jesus
- Know that you are seated in heavenly places
- Know that you have heaven's backing
- Know that you have charge over the angels

Therefore if any man be in Christ, he is a new creature; old things are passed away; behold, all things are become new. **2 Corinthians 5:17**

Authority

When identifying who you are in Christ, the advantage here is knowing you have the **same** authority as Christ to execute and expose the enemy. In **Matthew 7:29**, Jesus taught them as one having authority and not as the scribes or religious ruler.

Verily, verily, The hour is coming and now is, when the Dead shall hear the Voice of the Son of God: and they that hear shall live. For as the Father hath life in himself; so hath he given to the Son to have life in himself. And hath given him AUTHORITY to execute judgment also, because he is the Son of Man. **John 5:25-27**

Anointed

Christ is the Anointed One! The anointed one lives on the inside of us. Even when we don't know what we are anointed for, we are STILL anointed because Christ is on the inside. The very fact that Christ is in us should be an indication that our anointing will grow within the anointing of Christ. Our anointing will mature based on an intimate relationship with Christ.

> Hereby know that we dwell in him, and he in us, because he hath given us of his spirit. **1 John 4:13**

> And this is the confidence that we have in him, that if we ask, we know that we have the petitions that we desired of him. **1 John 5:14**

Knowing who you are through the anointing on your Church:

It is important to know the anointing and the assignment on your church and your leaders in order to help identify your anointing. This is crucial, especially if you believe that God has assigned you to a particular church to be developed under a particular leadership. Most times, you are assigned to a specific ministry to be developed in the anointing that is on your life. For example, some ministries have an anointing for singers and worshippers. Another ministry might have an anointing for wealth. Yet while another ministry may have an apostolic-prophetic anointing. At some point on your journey, God will lead you to a place to grow and flourish in the area of your particular anointing. **You must understand, that what is on the house is on you.** Now let me just say, this occurs at a mature place in your walk with Christ. You must go through the development of your salvation and walk out your sanctification to get to the point of purpose.

You need to know the:

- **Anointing** of your church
- **Assignment** of your church
- **Aim** of your church

Behold, how good and how pleasant it is for brethren to dwell together in unity; it is like the precious ointment upon the head, that ran down upon the beard, even Aaron's beard; that went down to the skirts of his garments; As the dew of Hermon, and as the dew that descended upon the mountains of Zion; for there the Lord commanded the blessing, even life for evermore. **Psalms 133:1-3**

PROPHETIC DECLARATIONS:

I declare that I accept and I embrace who God formed me to be even before the foundation of the world. Jeremiah 1:4-10

*I declare that I **do not** walk in confusion concerning my call, my gifts or my anointing.*

I declare that I understand how my identity increases my effectiveness and authority as a sniper

I declare that first and foremost, my identity and authority in in Jesus Christ. 1 John 4:13

I declare that my identity is for the building up of kingdom.

In Jesus' Name! Amen.

CHAPTER 4

HANDS ON TRAINING

As for God , his way is perfect, the word of the Lord is tried: he is a buckler to all them that trust in him. For who is God, save the Lord? And who is a rock, save our God. God is my strength and power: and he maketh my way perfect. He maketh my feet like hinds feet; and setteth me upon my high places. He teacheth my hands to war; so that a bow of steel is broken by mine arms. —**Psalm 18:30-34**

~

There is a season on the journey to becoming a prophetic sniper that training will ***only*** come by the Holy Spirit. There are specific strategies and developments that can only be downloaded directly from God. This divine training will bring a greater revelation to the sniper's anointing in order to effectively take the enemy out. We can look at David's life before he eliminated Goliath. David went through several levels of warfare in order to develop the warrior within him while he was guarding sheep. He contended with a lion and a bear before encountering Goliath. Each encounter represented a different level. Each level worked to develop the warrior within David.

David said to Saul, "Let no one lose heart on account of this Philistine; your servant will go and fight him."[33] Saul replied, "You are not able to go out against this Philistine and fight him; you are only a young man, and he has been a warrior from his youth."[34] But David said to Saul, "Your servant has been keeping his father's sheep. When a lion or a bear came and carried off a sheep from the flock, [35] I went after it, struck it and rescued the sheep from its mouth. When it turned on me, I seized it by its hair, struck it and killed it. [36] Your servant has killed both the lion and the bear; this uncircumcised Philistine will be like one of them, because he has defied the armies of the living God. [37] The LORD who rescued me from the paw of the lion and the paw of the bear will rescue me from the hand of this Philistine." Saul said to David, "Go, and the LORD be with you." **I Samuel 17:32-34**

The Season of the Sheep anointing

Sheep are meek animals. They are usually very quiet and gentle, holding themselves aloof from the world. In a herd, all sheep tend to listen to their leaders and they show esteem to them. Because of their obedient character, sheep are among the most popular animals beloved by mankind.

Jesus often compared us to sheep in the Bible, **John 10:27, My sheep hear my voice, and I know them, and they follow me.** He informed Simon Peter more than once to feed his sheep in **John 21:16 and John 21:17**; therefore sheep are very important to Jesus. David was trained on how to handle sheep **in the wilderness.** When you care for something for a while you begin to develop a love for what you are caring for. David took his job very seriously. He was placed over the sheep to **guard and protect them.** It was for this reason David developed a love for God's people and the decision was easy when it cam time for him fight for them in the time of battle against the uncircumcised Philistine, Goliath.

There is a season God will test your love for him and his people. He will place a person in your life to minister one on one about salvation and deliverance for their soul. If you can be faithful over that one assignment God gave you, he will begin to entrust you with more. He wants you to develop a love for his people because this will keep your passion alive, the love you have for one another; this will prove that you are his disciple indeed.

> A new commandment I give unto you, That ye love one another; as I have loved you, that ye also love one another.[35] By this shall all men know that ye are my disciples, if ye have love one to another. **John 13:34-35**

Moses went through a similar season as David where he developed love, compassion, and dedication for the sheep he was entrusted to care for while covering and protecting them. This is true training – to develop Christ's love for God's people. There must be a deep love for God's people in order to effectively war for them. Once this test has been passed, you are sure to graduate to the next level of warrior development.

The Season of the Lion anointing

Lions are a symbol of strength and courage. Lions have often been celebrated throughout history and cultures for these characteristics. Lions are also common symbols of royalty in some cultures. The phrase "king of the jungle" originated from ancient Egyptians who respected lions as war deities due to their strength, power and fierceness.

This season is necessary in order to build faith, strength (endurance) and courage. We have the **Lion of the tribe of Judah** within us, fighting and praying for us to get through our season of strength and power. The lion season is imperative for the warrior to develop and test strength and power in order to prevail.

What is power? It is the ability to act or produce an effect: a position of ascendancy over others or authority. **Psalms 62:11 says, God hath spoken once; twice have I heard this; that power belongeth unto God.** Therefore, God has given you power over the enemy which he cannot take. However, the enemy will give the *illusion* that this power will not work against his kingdom. This type of attack comes when it seems breakthrough will never happen. The counteracting tactic in this case is to **endure.** If the enemy can convince a believer to give up, then development in that place of authority or strength will never occur.

Looking unto Jesus the author and finisher of our faith; who for the joy that was set before him endured the cross, despising the shame, and is set down at the right hand of the throne of God. **Hebrews 12:2**

Prophetic snipers **must be bold as lions!** Let God arise and his enemies be scattered! Lions are:

- **Protective**
- **Brave**
- **Willing to fight**
- **Hunters**
- **Group members (part of a pride)**

Move in strength and power and take the enemy out! Do you know that a lion's roar can be heard from as far as five miles away? Open your mouth against the enemy and **ROAR!**

The lion hath roared, who will not fear? the Lord GOD hath spoken, who can but prophesy? **Amos 3:8**

The Season of the Bear anointing

A bear is much stronger than a man. In this respect, you must understand that you have more strength than your enemy. God will allow you to go through the season of the bear for more development so you will know and understand the actual strength you have within. There have been reports of human mothers, fueled by the concern and safety of their children, being strong enough to lift up cars in an effort to save their children and remove them out of harm's way. This is important to be sure of when the enemy comes in a way that makes you feel overpowered. Here is when the anointing from the bear season of development should overtake your spirit and cause you to **put on strength!**

I can remember very vividly going through this season of my life. It seemed as if the enemy's attacks were overwhelming. I was in a very hard season of warring against witches and warlocks; which were actually people who had deep envy and jealousy in their hearts. **Note:** when a person's heart is so overtaken with this kind of evil, they can become a potential witch in the spirit. When a person meditates with ill-wishes and ill-thoughts against another, it releases a spirit of sabotage and initiates an attack against the mind, anointing and destiny. This is also an example of a level of attack from powers and principalities (Ephesians 6). Here, you may contend against an actual principality in operation over a church or a region; especially if you operate in a governmental anointing (we will talk about this later). The purpose of these types of attacks are to cause a person to give up on what God has destined them to be in the kingdom and to give up on the assignment God has given them for that season. If we are going to walk in this new prophetic sniper's anointing, we must continuously obtain strategies from God for victory. Walking through the season of the bear helps us achieve a greater anointing for future assign -

ments. David once again prevailed over this type of attack with a bear, which helped him develop another level of anointing and strategy when he faced Goliath.

A bear's hearing ability is excellent and just like dogs, bears can hear high pitches that exceed human frequency ranges and sensitivity. Bears also see in color and have very good vision; similar to humans. If you're in this season, pray that you will also develop keen hearing and vision that will allow you to have the ability to hear and see the enemy from miles away.

The Season of Goliath's anointing

When we read the story of David in **1 Samuel 17,** we witness the fact that David went through various levels of development on his journey to becoming God's warrior. Because of his development, when he eventually faced Goliath (a principality type), he had strategy, he exuded confidence, skill and he was able to conquer this enemy effortlessly. **The Goliath season is a season of walking into a conquering anointing.**

After enduring this level of development, a sniper can walk in a room, not open their mouth and whatever prevailing spirit is ruling a certain atmosphere will begin to dismantle. The Goliath season is simply a season of walking in an effortless, dismantling authority with the assurance that you have the power to overcome any level of demonic force. **The sniper's anointing WILL arise!**

Breaking the Spirit of Fear

The primary weapon the enemy uses against a prophetic sniper is **fear**. When there is a strong anointing on your life to war against the kingdom of darkness, the enemy will dispatch certain phobias and spirits of fear. The enemy knows that he can't defeat you in any other way, but he will attempt to **dismantle** and **discredit** your power and authority with defeated thoughts.

> For God hath not given us the spirit of fear; but of power, and of love, and of a sound mind. **2 Timothy 1:7**

> God doesn't want us to be shy with the gifts, but bold, loving and sensible. **2 Timothy 1:7 (MSG)**

Here is why it is important to maintain the "helmet of salvation" – it protects the mind against demonic thoughts of condemnation and fear. A sniper must **know** their spiritual authority and understand the divine access to God they have in order to walk in the boldness required to thwart the enemy's tactics in this area.

There are several ways the enemy may use fear against a developing sniper, especially when there has been process and the sniper may be sensitive to the supernatural and aware of the enemy's plan. The enemy will try to catch the prophetic sniper off guard and may attempt to attack the sniper while they are asleep. The sniper may awake in the middle of the night and be unable to move or breathe. The sniper may also experience other types of phobia attacks. There may even be a physical manifestation of a demonic spirit through the spirit realm (such as pulling, punching, scratching, biting, bed shaking, etc.) – a tactic used by the enemy to cause a fear of the dark. Beloved, know that even in all this, **no weapon formed shall prosper!**

Everyone **may not** experience these high level attacks and not to this magnitude, but perhaps they may have experienced something similar. Prophetic Sniper, you must know that God has allowed this level of training. It is there to develop and not harm. The enemy's goal is only an illusion.

Illusion is another tactic to cause the sniper to believe the enemy has more power then he actually has. God's aim is that the sniper develop "spiritual muscles" and can stand firm in their authority.

> For though we walk in the flesh, we do not war after the flesh: for the weapons of our warfare are not carnal, but mighty through God to the pulling down of strong holds; casting down imaginations, and every high thing that exalteth itself against the knowledge of God, and bringing into captivity ever thought to the obedience of Christ. **2 Corinthians 10:3-5**

PROPHETIC ACTIVATION:

Lord, I thank you for this time of training. I thank you for trusting me to endure this process for your glory. I decree and declare that what you have graced me to endure for training, you will provide clarity and revelation. I will walk in another level of boldness to complete this task. I decree and declare that I will stay the course until the Holy Spirit has finished his workmanship in me. I thank you now that hands-on-training is working for my good.

In Jesus' Name. Amen!

CHAPTER 5

THE POSITION AND ANOINTING
OF THE SNIPER

*But unto every one of us is given grace according to the
measure of the gift of Christ.* – **Ephesians 4:7 KJV**

~

**A military sniper's primary function in warfare is to
provide detailed survey of the enemy's territory from a
concealed position and if necessary, reduce the enemy's
fighting ability by striking high value targets; especially
officers, communication, and other personnel.** This gives the
spiritual revelation that a sniper has to be in a place where the
enemy cannot "trace" them. They must be invisible. A sniper
even wears camouflage and field craft; which is also a tactic used
to hide in a concealed place, often times in plain sight. This
tactic is crucial; especially if a sniper's assignment is to
contend with high-ranking demons.

A sniper's **position and depth** in God will determine what level of
demons their anointing is graced to fight. Everyone is not assigned
to contend with this level of demonic activity. Again, a sniper must
spiritually graduate to this level – as we have mentioned in
previous chapters. As it is in the natural, so it is in the spirit. In the
military, soldiers must complete successful training at other levels
before moving to the next level of rank. God will not put more on
you than you can bear.

The Position of the Sniper

A sniper's position is in Christ. We live, move and have our being in Christ. If you are not in Christ, you **will not** have authority. Snipers do not walk in their own strength, but they walk in the strength of the Lord.

> And he raised us up together with him and made us sit down together, giving us joint seating with him(Jesus) in the heavenly sphere (by virtue of our being) in Christ Jesus (The anointed One). **Ephesians 2:6 AMP**

Scripture declares that we have been raised with Christ. This means that when Jesus got up with ALL power, we got up with him. Because we were raised with him, we have access to God through our relationship with Christ. We have POWER! We sit together with him at the right hand of the Father, so that means we also have AUTHORITY! The revelation here is that we war from a position in him and we should always remember that the Greater One lives on the inside of us!

The Place of the Sniper

Snipers have a *sure* hiding place. It is a protective place of refuge, restoration, and refilling. It is also an intimate place of communion. It is a concealed place out of the enemy's line of sight. As prophetic snipers, we must know there is a concealed place that exists where the enemy cannot trace or find us.

> He that dwelleth in the secret place shall abide under the shadow of the almighty. I will say unto the Lord, he is my refuge and my fortress and my God, in him will I trust. He shall cover thee with his feathers, and under his wings shalt thou trust; his truth shall be thy shield and buckler. **Psalms 91:1-4 KJV**

43

The "path" to this concealed, secret place is through intimacy and worship to God. There is a blueprint to follow in order to tap into the heart of his presence. We must have a clean heart to ascend to this place in God.

> Who shall ascend into the hill of the Lord? Or who shall stand in his holy place? He that hath clean hands and a pure heart; who hath not lifted up his soul unto vanity, nor sworn deceitfully. He shall receive the blessing from the Lord, and righteousness from the God of his salvation. This is the generation of them that seek him, that seek thy face, o Jacob. Selah. **Psalms 24:3-6 KJV**

An effective sniper should always have a hunger and a thirst for the next level in God. **John 7:38 says, he that believeth on me, as the scripture hath said, out of his belly shall flow rivers of living waters**. Something *must* be in the sniper's belly in order to keep them constantly seeking God's presence. The Father would have it no other way.

The Place of Righteousness

Righteousness in the Greek means integrity, virtue, purity of life, and correctness in thinking. There are seasons where the sniper will have to prove their walk in the kingdom to ensure that it couples with the gift and anointing of the sniper.

> Blessed are they which do hunger and thirst after righteousness: for they shall be filled. **Matthew 5:6 KJV**

Distrust is at an all time high concerning unbelievers and the church. The gifts and callings of God are without repentance; therefore, unbelievers must see a difference in the life of the believer. If believers conform to the ways and habits of unbelievers, it brings the word of God to no effect. A sniper's integrity MUST be in alignment with the word of God.

Conforming to God's word is truly a process. But when unbelievers are watching and are expecting kingdom believers to be examples of how to walk out his word, we must be very sensitive to convictions that do not line up with his word.

Because of the next level anointing we are preparing to walk in, we cannot give a place to the devil and allow him the opportunity to discredit our anointing. The Bible says that he roams as a roaring lion seeking whom he may devour. **Do not be the stumbling block to someone else's deliverance!** You might be the only witness of Jesus they will encounter.

> Be sober, be vigilant; because your adversary the devil, as a roaring lion, walketh about, seeking whom he may devour.
> **1 Peter 5:8 KJV**

The place of righteousness is key to moving into a deeper and closer place of intimacy with God. The righteousness of Christ penetrates the darkness that may hinder attaining an inner place in him. Here is where the power of Christ is able to sharpen your discernment; which causes more clarity in the spirit realm. **This all stems from a personal relationship with Christ.**

Ignorance of God's righteousness can detour one into their own "idea" of what righteousness is to God. One can begin to filter and perceive through the soul instead of the spirit.

> Brethren, my heart's desire and prayer to God for Israel is, that they might be saved. For I bear them record that they have a zeal of God, but not according to knowledge. For they being ignorant of God's righteousness, and going about to establish their own righteousness, have not submitted themselves unto the righteousness of God. **Romans 10:1-7 KJV**

The Place of Destiny

A sniper should have a longing for destiny or the divine purpose for which they were created. Destiny is something which a person or thing has been created for or what they have been created to do before the foundations of the world. Having an awareness about the fact that *every* believer has destiny provides better understanding of specific prayer mantle or mantles. It also provides better understanding of prayer targets for more effectiveness in prayer assignments. For example: you may have an anointing to shift youth to a place of having better self-esteem; you may have an anointing to pray for leaders; or you may have an anointing to shift people and atmospheres to their next level spiritually. Whenever there is a passion or concern with God, he will give you revelation concerning your prayer mantle, prayer assignments, and prayer target.

> The Lord will perfect that which concerneth me; thy mercy, o Lord endureth forever; forsake not the works of thine own hands. **Psalms 138:8 KJV**

> I know what I'm doing. I have it all planned out, plans to take care of you, not abandon you, plans to give you the future you hope for. When you call on me, when you come and pray to me, I'll listen. When you come looking for me, you'll find me. Yes, when you get serious about finding me and want it more than anything else. I'll make sure you won't be disappointed." God's decree. **Jeremiah 29:11-14 MSG**

Sniper's prayers should do 3 things in their spiritual walk:

1) It will PROVOKE

I consider this *outer court posture*. Outer court posture is the place of sacrifice. Here is where flesh comes under submission and it is crucified. This posture in his presence should provoke the flesh to line up to the voice and will of

God. The sniper's spirit should be sold out enough to say, "Lord I will give it all up, just to have you and the will of God for my life." The outer court place is also a realm of warring because there may still be a fight concerning issues with the flesh.

> And now Lord, what wait I for? My hope is in thee. Deliver me from all my transgressions; make me not the reproach of the foolish. **Psalms 39:7-8 KJV**

> But I keep under my body and bring it into subjection: lest that by any means, when I have preached to others, I myself should be a castaway. **1 Corinthians 9:27 KJV**

2) It will PUSH

This is the *inner court posture* in his presence. Here is the place where praise will erupt out of us because the pressure is now on to **push pass** the past and any current situations. In this position, you will either die or push your way to the next level in God. This posture may birth a new song out of your spirit, a new dance or even new tongues. This is also a place of waiting on God because at times, when burdened with life's pressures it can be hard to stand still and wait. However, when you learn to push pass feelings, endurance is birthed and you now begin to walk in the anointing to **push through!** Believe it or not, this process also develops another level of faith. The next time the sniper enters this place of prayer for a person, place or thing, the muscle of prayer is now developed.

As mentioned earlier, *inner court posture* is also a place where patience is often tested. In this posture, God will often "hide" from us to see if we will wait for him or if we will wait long enough for the prayer target or assignment to complete or break. Cycles of waiting and pushing is God's way of building and developing the sniper's faith in him and increasing spiritual muscles; thereby producing more effective prayers.

> Lord, by thy favor thou hast made my mountain to stand strong: thou didst hide thy face, and I was troubled. I cried to thee, o Lord; and unto the Lord I made supplication. **Psalms 30:7-8 KJV**
>
> Verily thou art a God that hidest thyself, O God of Israel, the Saviour. **Isaiah 45:15 KJV**

3) It will PROMOTE

Here we have entered the *holy of holies posture*. This is the **place where promotion in faith occurs**. The sniper has now graduated to the place where the enemy is unable to find or trace them because they have been engulfed in his presence!

> You who sit down in the High God's presence, spend the night in Shaddai's shadow, Say this: "GOD, you're my refuge. I trust in you and I'm safe!" That's right—he rescues you from hidden traps, shields you from deadly hazards. His huge outstretched arms protect you—under them you're perfectly safe; his arms fend off all harm. Fear nothing—not wild wolves in the night, not flying arrows in the day, Not disease that prowls through the darkness, not disaster that erupts at high noon. Even though others succumb all around, drop like flies right and left, no harm will even graze you. You'll stand untouched, watch it all from a distance, watch the wicked turn into corpses. Yes, because GOD's your refuge, the High God your very own home, Evil can't get close to you, harm can't get through the door. **Psalms 91:1-7 MSG**

In this posture, all flesh has died and the sniper has now pushed past the waiting on God – they have now entered the secret place. The sniper has made it to the keeping realm of God's presence. This is the realm of no more fighting.

The sniper has now encountered God's nature of **Jehovah Gibbor**, which means "the God that defends". God himself is fighting now and all the sniper has to do is stand still and see his salvation!

PROPHETIC DECLARATIONS:

I declare that I will remain in an elevated place in God so that I may walk out his Righteousness. Psalm 24:3

I declare that I will walk into my complete place of destiny.

I declare that I will remain aware of the sniper's position. Psalm 91:1

I will submit to my process of intercessory development from the place of outer court posture to the holies of holies posture.

I declare that I will endure through and press through keeping my focus on God. Psalms 30:7-8

I declare a never-ending hunger and thirst for the presence of God. Matthew 5:6

In Jesus' Name!

CHAPTER 6

BIRTHING OUT THE CHURCH THROUGH PRAYER

Verily, verily, I say unto you, Except a corn of wheat fall into the ground and die, it abideth alone: but if it die, it bringeth forth much fruit. – **John 12:24**

~

Today, the Body of Christ is in desperate need of prophetic snipers that will stand as watchmen for this end-time move of God. Many believe that the church is simply waking up on Sunday, putting on their Sunday's best and just going to a building to hear the choir, announcements and the preacher. However, when there is a particular "body" or ministry that has specifically made space in the spirit as fertile ground in order for God to download a seed (an assignment) for a move to occur in the earth, here is a ministry that is now ready to be birthed out. If there is no seed in the womb of the spirit, nothing can be impregnated in order for something to be developed and ultimately birthed out.. **John 12:24 states, verily, verily I say unto you, except a corn of wheat fall into the ground and die, it abideth alone, but if it dies, it brings**

forth much fruit. Here is where the prophetic sniper has to receive the vision and assignment of the ministry and region in order to help push and birth out. In Chapter 9, we will go further in detail about how intercessors are supposed to assist the visionary spiritually in order to help accomplish their assignment in the region or territory.

In the beginning, Holy Spirit is the birther and he births through willing vessels. Here is why the Bible states in **Isaiah 59:16** that "God wondered that there was no intercessor". The Bible goes on to say, "so he himself stepped in to save them with his strong arm, and his justice sustained him". Therefore the Spirit can birth or bring forth in the earth.

Genesis 1:1-2 also declares, **in the beginning the earth was without form and void.** The words "without form" is the Hebrew word *tohuw* which means a desolation; to lie waste, a desert, empty (barren). The basic concept is lifeless or in other words, no life. In verse 2, the Spirit of God **moved** upon the face of the waters. The Hebrew word used for moved is *rachap* which literally means "to brood over". Webster describes brood as an off spring; progeny or that which is bred or produced. In other words the Holy Spirit was birthing or bringing forth life – in the beginning.

This confirms that we are vessels for the Holy Spirit, just as Mary was used to birth out the "Chief Cornerstone" (Jesus). In **Luke 1:34** and **35**, the Holy Spirit overshadowed Mary which also supported and gave her the strength to birth out this new move in the earth. We must always be sync with and available to partner with the Holy Spirit in order for him to work through us. **Phil 2:13 KJV** states that **for it is God which worketh in you both to will and to do of His good pleasure**.

Understanding that snipers are birthers for God, the Holy Spirit wants to bring forth heaven's agenda through us. **John 7:38** declares that **from his innermost being shall flow rivers of living water**. Innermost here is the word *koilia* which means "womb". We are the womb of God on earth.

In order for the church to birth out, the prophetic birther must go through a season of travail. The Body of Christ will often use this word lightly because of the definition Webster gives – "painful work", exertion, toil, agony, or to labor hard. **No one wants to work**. The harvest is truly plenteous, but the laborers are few (**Matthew 96:37-38**). The Lord goes on the say, "pray for the labourers". Travail in Hebrew means to give birth or to bring forth. Emphasis here is on the spiritual power released to give birth spiritually and not the physical which may accompany the act of travailing (groaning, weeping, crying). Most of us who are acquainted with travailing prayer have made what happens physically the focus; thereby missing the spiritual significance which is the evidence that something is being born of the Spirit.

Spiritual travail – A level of intensity marked by a Holy Spirit burden to actually bring to pass something through prayer. This could be a given promise; a prophetic insight or a Holy Spirit illuminated need in a person, church, city or nation.

Examples of Spiritual Travail:

In **I Kings 18:41-45,** we can see Elijah's posture in this passage is that of a woman giving birth. We can say that Elijah was actually in a travailing (birthing) prayer

This kind of prayer can often be agonizing and heavy. The prayer is literally helping to "pull" something that exists in a spiritually realm into a physical, actualized place. Even though it was God's will to bring the rain and it was also God's time for rain, God still needed a vessel on earth to receive the prophetic download and birth the plans of God out in prayer and release the rain of the Spirit or the move of God. **James 5:16** also refers to this event and calls it "fervent prayer".

Simeon. Luke 2:25-34. Simeon waited in prayer and expectation until Jesus (the Savior) was born. He did not want to die until he saw it. Snipers should also have the same level of tenacity. Snipers should want to see the manifestation of God's vision. This helps the sniper to remain faithful in prayer and properly positioned in birthing mode.

Prophetess Anna. **Luke 2:36-38**. Anna was in the temple night and day until redemption came to Jerusalem. This is a form of labor and work. Anna was laboring around the clock for the deliverance of Jerusalem.

Christ's Travail. John 11:33-38; 41-43. Before Jesus called Lazarus forth, each verse spoke about a stirring, trouble, and travail in his spirit before he got to the tomb. Verse 33 says that Jesus was deeply moved and troubled, which means he was moved with indignation. The word trouble here is *tarasso* which means to stir up or to agitate. Jesus was stirring up the anointing within himself before he even got to the tomb and then the Spirit brought forth in him.

When Jesus was in the Garden of Gethsemane (**Matt 26:36-39**), he endured another level of travail for the redemption of humanity. Here, he was in labor and the Bible states Jesus began to shed great drops of blood. Yes, even Jesus had to birth the will of God in the earth.

> They that sow in tears shall reap in joy. He that goeth forth and weepeth, bearing precious seed, shall doubtless come again with rejoicing, bringing his sheaves with him. **Psalms 126:5, 6 KJV**

In order for a prophetic sniper to have the type of faith that can assist with birthing out a church, their faith must be:

Tested/Tried. This means to put to trial, to be examined, to inspect closely; to test the quality, value, or usefulness. In other words, what you are made of? Are you withdrawing from God because he is not coming through when you thought he should ? Are you going to leave the kingdom because it's not as easy as it was in the world? Snipers must always *dare* to believe God on every level.

> That the trial of your faith, being much more precious than of gold that perisheth, though it be tried with fire, might be found unto praise and honour and glory at the appearing of Jesus Christ: **I Peter 1:7 KLV**
>
> Beloved, think it not strange concerning the fiery trial which is to try you, as though some strange thing happened unto you: But rejoice, inasmuch as ye are partakers of Christ's sufferings; that, when his glory shall be revealed, ye may be glad also with exceeding joy. **1 Peter 4:12-13**

This is GOD's Word on the subject: "As soon as Babylon's seventy years are up and not a day before, I'll show up and take care of you as I promised and bring you back home. I know what I'm doing. I have it all planned out—plans to take care of you, not abandon you, plans to give you the future you hope for. When you call on me, when you come and pray to me, I'll listen. When you come looking for me, you'll find me.Yes, when you get serious about finding me and want it more than anything else, I'll make sure you won't be disappointed." GOD's Decree. I'll turn things around for you. I'll bring you back from all the countries into which I drove you"—GOD's Decree—"bring you home to the place from which I sent you off into exile. You can count on it. **Jeremiah 29:11-14 MSG**

Tailored. To make or fashion as the work of a tailor. To make or adapt to suit a special purpose. God has a situation tailored just for you that is suited for you. No one else is designed to go through what you have gone through or what you are going through. It is destined for you because God is trying to get a unique anointing out of you that only YOU can operate in because it is ONLY YOU that has gone through the process.

Tamed. To bring perspective to your faith for the kingdom. Subdue and humble one's self knowing that everything you have been through is for the kingdom. A sniper must understand that the warfare experienced (past, current, future) is for the building up of God's kingdom. Our faith is not just for us but others.

Humble yourselves, therefore, under God's mighty hand, that he may lift you up in due time. Cast all your anxiety on him because he cares for you. Be alert and of sober mind. Your enemy the devil prowls around like a roaring lion looking for someone to devour. 9 Resist him, standing firm in the faith, because you know that the family of believers throughout the world is undergoing the same kind of sufferings.And the God of all grace, who called you to his eternal glory in Christ, after you have suffered a little while, will himself restore you and make you strong, firm and steadfast. To him be the power for ever and ever. Amen. **1 Peter 5:6-10 NIV**

There are obstacles snipers will encounter before birthing comes forth. They are:

Birth Controllers. People who are used by the enemy to regulate or prevent a birth from manifesting. There are always witches, warlocks, and the spirit of Jezebel dispatched to stop a prophetic birth (a move of God) from breaking forth. Birth controllers are sent to stop progression. Birth controllers observe the ministry in an attempt to locate a "sensitive" place (gates – we will discuss in Chapter 9) within the ministry. Birth controllers love to flock to the areas of prayer, worship and any vicinity near the leaders or the pillars of a ministry. Prayer and worship mainly because these ministries are the most important ministries when God is seeking to birth something new. Birth controllers are vessels for the kingdom of darkness.

For our struggle is not against flesh and blood, but against the rulers, against the authorities, against the powers of this dark world and against the spiritual forces of evil in the heavenly realms. Therefore put on the full armor of God, so that when the day of evil comes, you may be able to stand your ground, and after you have done everything, to stand. **Ephesians 6:12-13**

Birth Defects. An abnormal condition that may occur to a baby. The defect may be present in the structure or function of some part of the baby's body. In the Body of Christ and in churches, if the apostolic ministry is not functioning with order and a prophetic eye, we will begin to place people in positions where they should not be. In the long run, improper positioning may cause birth defects within the ministry and within individuals. This may occur in the form of no or slow progression within a ministry's growth, an onset of carnality and worldliness, underdevelopment, premature deaths, accidents and incidents, and etc.

We must persist in praying that the Holy Spirit continues to guide our leaders to appoint people where they have been anointed for and in positions they have the capacity and competence for (both naturally and spiritually); and not just because they are familiar with them in the flesh. In **1 Corinthians 12**, God ordained that we must set gifts in the body where they belong, so the Body (church or ministry) can function properly and to its fullest extent.

For the birth of a healthy church, we as prophetic snipers must always pray for:

The Apostle or Prophet (Pastor, Sr. Leader) of the House

Prophetic snipers at *all cost*, must protect the visionary of the house. We will go further in detail concerning this in chapter 8. If the enemy can blind the eyes of the visionary, then there **will be no vision**. Without a vision the people will perish. God has anointed intercessors that have the *grace* to cover the senior leader(s). Prophetic snipers who can be trusted. Everyone **is not** called to this sensitive level of intercession. Snipers at this level must be skilled and trained spiritually to flow and function as prophetic snipers here. These individuals must have a discipline of fasting and prayer. They must have healthy eating habits and drink plenty of water to maintain their body for this level warfare. At this level God has to:

1. Trust You

2. Test you

3. Tame You

The Power of the House

Prophetic snipers must stay on their post(s) in order to prepare and ensure the atmosphere is conducive for the move of God. There are times where God will begin to shift in every service and prophetic snipers must maintain this atmosphere through prayer and declaring his will at that moment. This allows the glory and the presence of the Lord to rest and abide until his work is complete. We have to protect the presence and the power of God at all cost, because in his presence is the fullness of joy, deliverance, healing and breakthroughs for the people of God. Prophetic snipers must have a desire for the presence of God. There are intercessors anointed for worship that will have this passion and strategy to assist in the spirit. This anointing is *especially* needed when deliverance, healing and miracles are going forth.

> One thing have I desired of the Lord, that will I seek after, that I may dwell in the house of the Lord all the days of my life, to behold the beauty of the Lord, and to inquire in his temple. **Psalm 27:4**

The People of the House (or Region)

Prophetic snipers must contend to keep the people of God covered from the plans and plots of the enemy.

> How good and pleasant it is when God's people live together in unity! It is like precious oil poured on the head, running down on the beard, running down on Aaron's beard, down on the collar of his robe. It is as if the dew of Hermon were falling on Mount Zion. For there the LORD bestows his blessing, even life forevermore. **Psalms 133:1-3 NIV**

Snipers must continuously pray for people's deliverance and must remain accountable to the person whom God lays on the sniper's heart to pray for. Snipers must continuously declare unity, love and peace. **God cannot birth or work properly through a church when there is strong discord.** Snipers assigned to accomplish this task must have a love for the people of God.

Graced for the Assignment

There are certain snipers assigned and mantled for a particular church. When you are a prophetic sniper, you are not just called to pray. You are mandated with assignments from heaven to pray the will of the Lord on earth. You are mandated to sacrifice and remain in God's presence so he may reveal the good, the bad and the ugly; knowing that he will provide the necessary grace to walk out the process and he will release the wisdom and power to carry out a particular assignment. God just needs a humble, sold out vessel to birth out his mind and heart in the earth.

But he giveth more grace, wherefore he saith, God resisteth the proud, but giveth grace to the humble. **James 4:6**

Let us therefore come boldly unto the throne of grace, that we may. obtain mercy, and find grace to help in the time of need. **Hebrews 4:16**

When the assignment seems unbearable, God will grant the grace to press through and reach beyond the break. A sniper's love and intention to please God will cause them to complete the assignment he has given them for that particular ministry, person, place or thing.

In **John 14:15-16** it states **that if you love me, keep my commandments**; which means that what I have told you in my word and also what I have downloaded in your spirit (through prayer).

When a sniper is graced with a mandate of prayer from God, the warfare of the assignment will try to bring bitterness in an effort to cause distraction about what God is teaching at that moment. However, the living word must flow out of the sniper's belly which declares **"not my will but your will be done"**! Just as it is in a natural birth, there are pains and complications a mother experiences along the process of birthing a new baby. Pains can often start at the onset of the 1st trimester. This may also parallel a church or ministry spiritually when it is in the 1st trimester of growth which is the "birthing stage". Each level of growth in the ministry will develop the prophetic sniper simultaneously because it will cause the sniper to grow more sensitive to enemy plots and plans for that particular ministry.

Often times, the enemy usually comes cyclically; in the same way, but may manifest in different forms.

In each level of growth, the prophetic sniper will have the ability to:

Examine the enemy. This means to inspect very intimately and closely. Understand that a sniper is aware of every move of his enemy. He knows almost accurately the enemy's next step or move. We must study the pattern of how the enemy operates in our home, church, marriage, etc. Here is where a sniper may have to change up strategy on how to defeat the enemy in different seasons.

Expose the enemy. Expose means to bring to light or to cause to be open to view. A sniper must know his enemy in order to expose every trap and evil way of the enemy. Spiritually, a sniper must be able to skillfully expose his moves, his attacks, his discords, his agents and every vessel that attempts to come in his name. A sniper must expose every demon of flattery, seduction and witchcraft that will try to hinder the growth of the person or the progression of a ministry.

Expel the enemy. In the Greek, expel means "to cast out" or "to send away". This happens once a sniper has examined and exposed the enemy and now it is time to obtain strategy about how to cast him out.

Lastly, snipers must be vessels that are sanctified, sacrificial and sold out in order to endure an assignment through to its completion.

> But in a great house, there are not only vessels of gold and silver, but also of wood and of the earth and some to honour and some to dishonor. If a man therefore purge himself from these, he shall be vessels unto honour, sanctified and meet for the Master's use and prepared for every good work. **2 Timothy 2:20-21**

Sanctified vessels. Vessels that are consecrated and set apart for a holy assignment. Vessels that are devoted solemnly to a purpose are declared sacred. Intercessors must be vessels set aside for God to use. Not that intercessors should think of themselves as "a great wonder", but it should be understood that snipers have given themselves completely for the master's use.

> Then Joshua said to the people, "Sanctify yourselves [for His purpose], for tomorrow the LORD will do wonders (miracles) among you. **Joshua 3:5**

Sacrificial vessels. The offering of something precious to deity or something offered in sacrifice. This may include your time, spirit, body, and heart for the Holy Spirit to work through. Snipers must be sacrificial lambs and must be willing to die to their own wants and even needs for the will of God. For example, it can be a beautiful weekend and everyone else is going to the mall. God may speak to a sniper and say "I need you to stay at home today and get in my presence so that my spirit can move freely in service on Sunday". Intercessors must be sensitive to the voice of the Lord and they must be obedient to the Spirit's leading. Snipers understand that their disobedience may hinder someone's breakthrough. **Hence: God sacrificed Jesus, his only Son for the purpose of humanity.** He was the ultimate sacrificial Lamb.

Sold out vessels. Snipers must be emptied out of "self" in order for God to download his will in the earth. Snipers must keep their spirits and hearts open towards heaven. Therefore, an intercessor's heart should be purged and washed from any offense, hurt, or disappointments – **this should be ongoing**. Snipers should be intentional about keeping their heart's pure so that the execution of God's plan is not interrupted or tainted. If the sniper is not in a place of purity of heart, their prayers can become tainted which can turn into witchcraft prayers. This leads to soul or "physic" prayers instead of praying out of purity of spirit and heart.

> Except the LORD build the house, they labour in vain that build it: except the LORD keep the city, the watchman waketh but in vain. **Psalms 127:1 KJV**

PROPHETIC ACTIVATION

Lord, I thank you now for the church. I thank you that as in Hebrews 10:25, I will not forsake the assembly of ourselves together and I will remember to exhort one another. I release and declare an anointing on the ministry you have placed me in to flourish. Thank you NOW for another level over my leaders, the vision of the house and the assignment of the house. I thank you now that my church will grow in ministry, mantles and MIRACLES!

In Jesus' Name. Amen!

CHAPTER 7

THE POWER OF THE WATCHMAN

I have set watchmen upon thy walls, O Jerusalem, which shall never hold their peace day nor night: ye that make mention of the Lord, keep not silence. — **Isaiah 62:6**

~

In this hour, the church is in dire need of strong, proven, trusted and anointed watchmen. These types of watchmen are *shamar prophets* — especially in an apostolic-prophetic ministry. The enemy may attack in various ways because there are no TRUE watchmen that are prophetically guarding gates in the spirit realm. The church is "sleeping with the enemy" on many different levels. In this kingdom hour, there are two major spirits fighting for supreme influence within the church: 1) the Spirit of Truth and 2) the spirit of perversion. **Truth and perversion have engaged in an ongoing fight to take absolute position in the kingdom of God.** Where truth reigns, perversion is constantly seeking to take territory, which creates counterfeits. A counterfeit spirit is an imitation of the authentic with a specific intent to deceive.

The Spirit of Truth *always* represents God. It will always point back to his word. The Spirit of Truth stands as a direct representative of God's word. If "it" (whatever *it* is) doesn't line up with the word of God, there is another spirit in operation.

> Howbeit when he, the Spirit of Truth is come, he will guide you into all truth: for he shall not speak of himself(self exaltation); but whatever he shall hear, that shall he speak and he will show you things to come prophetic. He shall Glorify Me: for he shall receive of mine and shall show it unto you. **John 16:13-14**

Again, the Spirit of Truth seeks to give God all glory. A person operating in this spirit will walk in a level of humility and will be very careful and sensitive about always exalting God and not themselves. A person operating in the spirit of Truth hates pride, religion, injustice and inauthenticity. They hate when God does not get glory. These people typically hate what God hates and love what God loves.

> The fear of the Lord is to hate evil; pride, and arrogancy, and the evil way, and the forward mouth, do I hate.
> **Proverbs 8:13**

The Spirit of Perversion represents the deception and confusion of the enemy; always pointing the attention back to himself instead of God. The spirit of perversion will twist the word of God and will "pretend" it represents God. Its motives are always for self-gain, self-promotion, self-exaltation – ultimately, they bring glory to themselves instead of God. Nebuchadnezzar was a good biblical example of refusing to give God glory for what he had done. Somewhere in Nebuchadnezzar's heart, he made the grave mistake of allowing the accomplishments he achieved to make him think *he* had actually built his empire.

The spirit of perversion is often very prideful, religious and manipulative because there is nothing in them that stand on truth. The truth is not in them; therefore they must constantly scheme and manipulate in order to *look* and *act* like truth. **Perversion can only act out what others have walked out and have obtained in the spirit of truth.** There is no real, true power or authenticity.

> For such are false apostles, deceitful workers, transforming themselves into the apostles of Christ -And no marvel; for Satan himself is transformed into an angel of light -Therefore it is no great thing if his ministers also be transformed AS ministers of righteousness; whose end shall be according to their works. **2 Corinthians 11:13-15**

This is why the watchmen's anointing is vitally crucial in this hour. The **watchmen's anointing** is the grace to hedge about (as with thorns), to guard, to protect, to watch, and to keep. This is a protective element of an apostolic-prophetic ministry. The watchmen's anointing is essential to guarding the spiritual GATES!

Where are the gatekeepers? Especially in the late hour of the night which is the enemy's favorite time to conspire. The *witching hour* (from 12AM – 3AM) is where snipers develop the most spiritual skill and precision. This duration of time is where the enemy always seeks to create new ways to execute old tricks.

Here is where discernment is sharpened and insight is illuminated concerning the enemy's tactics.

To guard can mean a number of things:

- to protect
- to watch over
- to stand guard over
- to police
- to secure
- to defend
- to shield
- to shelter
- to screen
- to cover

- to preserve
- to save
- to supervise
- to keep under surveillance
- or control
- to govern
- to restrain
- to suppress
- to be alert
- to take care

A watchmen's anointing and grace to flow should rest on the prophetic intercessor. This grace should come from the prophet or apostle of the house when you are *truly* connected to that house. **In Philippians 1:7, Paul said ye all are part-takers of my grace.** Your leader is the gate and overseer to that ministry. They have oversight concerning what goes in and out of the ministry. Therefore, in order for that leader to focus on the vision and assignment for the house, they can gracefully lay hands and transfer the watchmen's anointing to a person or people he or she trusts to execute a particular spiritual assignment for a particular ministry.

The local church is held up through pillars of the ministry. What exactly are pillars? These are vessels who have received the vision of the house and are strong and skilled enough to contend with the enemy and can stand strong **against his attacks against the ministry or assignment for the kingdom. Snipers represent a standard for God and for the ministry.** The standard will rise up in the sniper to engage and overcome any attack.

To keep a prophetic guard over the ministry, you must be:

1) **Strategic.** A sniper must always have a plan and strategy when engaging in war with the enemy. Most of the biblical characters in the bible either received divine instruction directly from God before engaging in any type of conflict or war. Or, they received instructions from someone in authority or from someone who had authority with God (i.e a prophet or king). David was an example of a man-of-war with a strategy. Johosephat was another example of someone who move forward with a divine plan.

2) **Skillful and Alert.** A sniper must have precision, skill, wisdom, and strong discernment when guarding over a ministry. A sniper must be able to understand the times and seasons of a particular ministry and to know *when* to pray *what* prayers. In military war, timing, skill, vigilance and precision **are all** extremely important when executing a strategy against an enemy.

3) **Strong.** A sniper must develop a strong anointing and strong spiritual anointing. In other words, a "devil don't play with me" attitude is necessary as a sniper. Therefore, a sniper must **overcome rejection, self-rejection** and **fear.** These enemies of the sniper must be replaced with strong identity and self-awareness in order to be able to guard effectively. **1 Peter 5:8 extols us to be sober, be vigilant; because your adversary the devil, is as a roaring lion, walking about seeking whom he may devour.** Here is the reason why we must keep guard over the flock: so the visionary can keep their eyes focused on the vision and the plan for ministry in kingdom.

The Leader and the Watchman

There are times when certain vessels partner up with ministries to sow seeds of destruction and seeds of discord for the purpose of distracting the ministry from God's will. The watchful (eagle eye) of the resident prophet(s) or key snipers can spot these vessels of dishonor and may release spiritual discomfort upon them so that they are *ill-at-ease* among the flock and can be quickly exposed. God's will is that none should perish, but that all would come into the knowledge of Christ. Therefore, once these vessels of dishonor are exposed and if they **refuse** restoration or deliverance so they can move into alignment with the overall vision of the house, they should leave that ministry through the apostolic leader who has the grace to release.

Hell has deployed certain spirits whose goal it is to target and undermine the overall growth, progression, and the ultimate destiny of a ministry. **The key spirit: Jezebel. Every leader should cooperate with the prophetic sniper(s) for strategies about exterminating this spirit from burgeoning, kingdom ministries.**

The Jezebel Spirit will ALWAYS seek to destroy and hinder the development of the prophetic ministry in a church or even a region and especially prophetic people. This spirit hates TRUE prophetic voices because it causes God's people to prosper in every way. It loves to take God's glory and wherever this spirit sees God moving, it lusts to be a part of that movement (wherever it is) to take the glory from God. Here is why **apostolic order is needed.** The Jezebel spirit hates order and authority. It loves to seduce by **flattery in order to gain power or** influence so it can control. Once the focus is on God, the Jezebel spirit tries to find ways to continuously glean attention – especially from leaders. **If the attention is on Jezebel then it is NOT on God.** This in turn produces idols and the birth of a fake, demonic and counterfeit system which is a **false apostolic**.

Jezebel will attempt to attack the prayer ministry to prevent snipers from taking them out. If it fails in this area, then like a snake it will employ tactics to discredit the snipers (i.e. labeling the sniper as crazy, a witch, witchy or weird). **However, in the name of balance, there are unhealthy, unprocessed, hurting intercessors who may be tainted.** It is extremely important that apostolic leader(s) understand the temperament, heart and warfare of the intercessor so they can properly rescue, recover, resuscitate or even remove the intercessor (if necessary). Effective snipers need a season of rest; they need covering, prayer, deliverance and healing. They need to be in the presence of the Lord. The Jezebel spirit causes churches to be guided more by the flesh rather than Holy Spirit. It loves to undermine people's ministries and destinies.

> Notwithstanding I have a few things against thee, because thou sufferest that woman Jezebel, which calleth herself a prophetess, to teach and to seduce my servants to commit fornication, and to eat things sacrificed unto idols. And I gave her space to repent of her fornication; and she repented not. **Revelation 2:20-21**

Ultimately, it loves to destabilize any divine order or instruction set by the apostle. Jezebel seeks to draw the entire church away from purity and divine assignment. It interferes with TRUE worship. When the Jezebel spirit is present, there will always be a hindrance to movement and progression, especially in an apostolic-prophetic ministry or even in the lives of apostolic-prophetic people. There will be a struggle moving with the current of Holy Spirit. It will cause ministries to stay in low, religious places where there is no portal of truth opened for God's glory.

Leaders, again it is very important to have strategy against Jezebel – if not, your ministry will be hindered. Jezebel is on a mission to devour apostolic-prophetic ministries and apostolic-prophetic people. The watchmen and the leader(s) should collaborate together to obliterate this enemy.

Examples of Watchmen

Elisha, 2 Kings 6:8-23

Elisha was a great example of a watchman in scripture; he was the ultimate watcher of the King; whenever the attack was conspiring against Israel. The anointing of a watchman would come upon Elijah and he would warn the King of the coming attack. The king was able to prepare and counteract the enemy before his plans went forth. This was such a setup of apostolic order because as soon as Elisha saw the attack in the spirit, he immediately went to the king to inform him. **Leaders listen!** You must allow space for *trusted, tested* and *proven* snipers to warn of impending danger. When this collaborative system is in place, leaders must be open to receive and willing to prepare. There should be a competent sniper positioned over your prayer ministry, or a prophet in the house that carries a sniper's anointing. There should be a prophetic person governing the prayer ministry gate.

This gate is very important to your ministry. There should be a balance in a sniper's anointing to see good and evil. **If there's a person on your team and all they see is evil, replace them quickly.** They should be in sync with what God is showing or speaking to the leader concerning the ministry. There is a season where the sniper should sit still to hear and receive the vision for the next level in the ministry and they should help the leader declare the next level. Again, Elisha had a heart for the king and the people. When he responded to what God was revealing, he was operating in the watchmen's anointing.

Simeon, Luke 2:25-33

Simeon was a great example of a watchman that was in a place of waiting on the promise of God. The blessing was actually promised to Israel. He had the tenacity to say "I will not die until I see this manifest and come to pass." Again, watchmen should also see blessings and not only evil. In Simeon's time, the promise was the Messiah, but Simeon prayed and consoled with Israel until he saw the promise come to pass.

Anna, Luke 2:36

Here we find a watchman who coupled her assignment with fasting and prayer while waiting on the promised Messiah. While waiting, she laid out before God and immersed herself in fasting and prayer until the promise came to pass. Leaders, make sure the person(s) you have appointed to any sensitive position has a disciplined life of fasting and praying; if not, they could be a hindrance to the vision, the assignment and the will of God. Sometimes, breakthrough can only occur with fasting and prayer as admonished in **Matthew 17:21.**

Requirements necessary to transition from intercessor to prophetic sniper:

1) **Higher level of a consecrated life.** To consecrate means to dedicate or set aside for a sacred purpose. This means one will devote whatever God has instructed them to sacrifice for the day, the week, the month, perhaps a year and maybe even a lifetime. This level of consecration allows a vessel to ascend to a place to hear God clearly for a dedicated purpose or assignment.

2) **Obedience to the logos and rhema word of God.** To purpose in one's heart to obey him completely allows a vessel to shift to another place in him. This means, anything that offends God in the vessel's life, they cut it off with the realization that "your" disobedience can cause someone or something to miss the breakthrough that God desires.

> And it shall come to pass, if thou shalt hearken diligently unto the voice of the Lord they God, to observe and to do all his commandments which I command thee this day, that the Lord they God will set thee on high above all nations of the earth: and all these blessings shall come on thee and overtake thee, if thou shalt hearken unto the voice of the Lord thy God. **Deuteronomy 28:1-2**

3) **The Eagle Eye.** The eagle has large eyes that are located on the sides of its head. Though the eagle's eyes are positioned in this way, it can still see straight ahead. The eagle has the keenest eyes of all birds which allows them to see their prey while soaring miles in the air. Catch this revelation: **in order to see with a keen eye in the spirit, you must ascend to an elevated place spiritually:**

PROPHETIC ACTIVATION:

Lord, give me the insight to see in the different realms of the spirit that I have been processed to see. Lord, I pray for the wisdom on how to carry this level and type of anointing. I pray your will in the earth now as you download your revelation concerning my ministry, my home and my church. I thank you NOW for the watchmen's anointing on my life.

In Jesus' Name, AMEN!

CHAPTER 8

THE COVERING OF LEADERS:
THE RULER SPIRIT

*For we wrestle not against flesh and blood, but against principalities, against powers, against the **rulers of the darkness** of this world, against spiritual wickedness in high places.* –
Ephesians 6:12

~

We have come to the most important chapter in this foundational manuscript because the enemy is looking to make true men and women of God fall completely out of his will. We are in an apostasy age (a great falling away) and if the enemy can ensnare the visionary, the gate of a ministry, or their assignment for the kingdom, he has consumed the entire body of that ministry. This is why it is so important to cover and protect the voice of the ministry (the visionary). There are also certain apostolic voices assigned to regions to execute God's will for that particular region which we will discuss in more detail in the following chapter.

The bible states in **Jeremiah 3:15, And I will give you pastors according to mine heart, which shall feed you with knowledge and understanding.** Therefore, the voice God has anointed for us should bring revelation to our lives. **Covering the voice of the leader must be a *primary focus*** when building an effective prayer strategy.

The church has become a laughing stock due to fallen leaders. This in turn has caused believers and non-believers alike to disrespect, dishonor or even devalue the mouthpieces of God across the body. As prophetic snipers, we should discern and sense when the voice, the vision, or the assignment is under attack. We understand that there are demonic forces in the air waves that will attempt to interrupt what God is saying or downloading to his people for these times.

There are high-level strategies that must be executed in order for heavenly downloads from God to be covered and protected effectively. If the enemy can discredit a God-appointed leader through deceit, delusion, distraction, impurity, carnality, worldliness, compromise, and etc., then he has accomplished his goal – **which is to ultimately strip the credibility and validity of God's mouthpieces.**

The Old Testament Mouthpiece. Jeremiah 1:4-5 and 8-10. v.4 Then the Word of the Lord came unto me saying, v.5   Before I formed thee in the belly, I knew thee; and before thou camest forth out of the womb, I sanctified thee, and I ordained thee a prophet unto the nations. v.8 Be not afraid of their faces; for I am with thee to deliver thee, saith the Lord. v.9 Then the Lord put forth his hand, and touched my mouth, and the Lord said unto me, Behold, I have put my words in thy mouth. v.10 See, I have this day set thee over the nations and over the kingdoms, to root out, and pull down, and to destroy, and to throw down, to build, and to plant.

New Testament Mouthpiece. Mark 1:2-4. v.1 As it is written in the prophets, Behold, I send my messenger before thy face, which shall prepare thy way before thee. v.2 The voice of one crying in the wilderness, prepare ye the way of the Lord, make his paths straight (This was said of John the Baptist the prophetic voice in the New Testament). Whereas in **v.4**, John baptized in the wilderness, and preached the baptism of repentance for the remission of sins.

Here, we have two characters of the bible which are Jeremiah, an Old Testament Prophet, and John the Baptist, a New Testament prophet. These two prophets had characteristics that described the voice of this time. Jeremiah name means "Yahweh lifts up" or "establishes". Some may contend that because of the harsh prophecies of Jeremiah, he was *only* obeying the voice of the Lord, which led to persecution and a time of weeping for the prophet. Jeremiah was a man divinely called by God (directly) in his youth from the priest city of Anathoth. He was a heartbroken prophet with a heartbreaking message to the stiff-neck people of Judah. Though Jeremiah was despised and persecuted by his own countrymen, Jeremiah bathed his harsh prophecies in tears of compassion because he was connected with the heart and mind of God.

As a New Testament mouthpiece, John the Baptist, whose name means "Yahweh is Gracious", in his day prepared the way for the Lord by blowing the trumpet for people to repent for their sins before the coming of the Lord. It was told by the Angel Gabriel that John was not to drink wine or any fermented drink, but that he would be filled with the "Holy Spirit" from birth and he would minister in the spirit and the power of the Prophet Elijah.

Covering the Voice

The voice of the leader in your ministries and regions has an assignment by God. As God told Jeremiah, "I put my words in your mouth" and for this reason, leaders must keep a reverence for God and his holy ordinances in order to be his true mouthpiece. As prophetic snipers, we must execute prayer strategies to keep the voice of God reserved and respected. Tactically speaking, we must pray that the voice is:

Acknowledged. This means to admit, discover and own. **Matthew 10:27** says, **"my sheep hear my voice and I know them and they follow me"**. Revelation exhorts **"He that hath an ear, let him hear what the Spirit saith unto the Churches"** As prophetic snipers, we must continue to pray that **God's people hear the spiritual voice of the Lord and not the natural voice of the leader.** We also must embody the notion that we own the voice. Meaning, we must understand the mouthpiece as the actual voice of the Lord speaking. We must constantly pray to never become so common or complacent with the natural voice that we "cloud out" the voice of Almighty God speaking through them from the Throne. Tactically speaking, we must pray over the spiritual ears of the people to hear God's voice.

Appreciated. We must value, honor and be grateful for the voice in our lives. God told **Jeremiah in 1:8, be not afraid of their faces for I am with you to deliver you.** He knew that people would not receive the word of the Lord (at times) with passion or with an urgency in their hearts – so he had to comfort Jeremiah. **Psalms 105:15** says, **"touch not mine anointed, and do my prophets no harm"**. This is not a physical harm. The word harm here in Hebrew means to displease, to bring or do evil to, to hurt, to vex, or to do worse. We have to pray that the hearers of the word value and appreciate the word daily.

In ministries, the people of God may develop a dull, spiritual ear (due to the cares of the world, issues in life and etc.) to the voice of the house; therefore, we must continue to pray that appreciation does not decrease. We must pray in every season the people receive new insight and constant refreshing.

Accepted. This means we must pray that the voice receives and is willing to agree and obey to *whatever* God is saying or instructing us to do as a body of believers. We must also continue to pray against becoming too familiar with the voice of the house. We must target immature believers and help them to understand that we do not handle the voice of our leader as our friend, our husband, or our natural father. Having the wrong perspective will interfere with our acceptance of the voice. **Hebrews 3:7 and wherefore as the Holy Ghost saith, Today if ye will hear his voice. Harden not your hearts, as in the day of temptation in the wilderness. Verse 11** says **we will not enter his rest**; therefore, as a prophetic body, we must keep our *prophetic ears* tuned to what God is speaking.

Affirmed. We must confirm, pray, and declare that whatever the prophetic voice says is what we say and whatever the voice speaks, we echo and execute. As a prophetic sniper, we must pray that there is agreement with the voice. If the voice declares and instructs that God has proclaimed a ministry-wide fast and consecration, snipers must be sure to cover what God has proclaimed and pray it through completely. Snipers must ensure to pray that the ministry comes into agreement, aligns to declarations, and is heading in the direction of what has already been released. **Amos 3:3** substantiates this statement by declaring, **"how can two walk together unless they be agreed?"**

Prophetic snipers have the ability and authority to pray for:

Restoration of the voice. Snipers can pray that God reestablish what was initially declared back to its original state.

Retaining the voice. Retain means to be kept in a fixed place or position. This means that snipers have the authority to declare that the voice of God remains fixed in the people's heart and spirit. This is necessary because there are demonic influences that seek to kill and suffocate the prophetic word and snatch every prophetic promise.

Releasing the voice. Snipers must declare the freedom of the voice from confinement or restraint to a local body or even a moment. Snipers must contend for what the voice has declared, announced, decreed or proclaimed. The voice **is not** limited to just to our local ministries, but they are assigned to regions, to cities, to the nation and to the world. We do an injustice to God and the voice when they are not released appropriately.

The Assignment of the Leader

The assignment of the leader concerning God's people is to shift them from one place to another. An assignment of the prophetic sniper to pray for transition to take place. The leader's purpose is to shift the people from a:

- **Familiar place to a Prophetic place**

- **Failing place to a Prosperous place**

- **Fighting place to a Peaceful place**

Covering the God-Man or God-Woman

Proverbs 29:2 declares **that when the righteous are in authority, the people rejoice: but when the wicked beareth rule, the people mourn.**

The set man or woman over a ministry or over a particular assignment for the kingdom of God is a major gate. This means that they are a major opening, passport, key, ticket to that particular assignment. It is one of the key areas prophetic snipers have been sanctioned to cover and must always include this in any prayer focus or strategy concerning the visionary and the house. The gate is one of the most important areas because if **the enemy is able to find a crack or opening within the gate, he understands he has access to the entire ministry and its people.** Prophetic snipers must walk in strong spiritual discernment and **only** move on what is revealed by the Holy Spirit and *not* assumptions.

Prophetic snipers must be able to guard and cover areas where leaders themselves (through no fault of their own) may walk in fear, rejection, vulnerability, unforgiveness, bitterness and etc., that may occur due to ongoing stresses and disappointments of the ministry. The very people of the ministry that leaders have been entrusted to lead may also be the source of these same hurts within the heart of the leaders. If these areas go any length of time without resolution, it may cause an opening within the "gate" that allows access for the enemy to infiltrate the ministry, its assignment, or its vision. Once the enemy sees an opportunity or a crack, he will definitely take full advantage of it in an attempt to accomplish his goal; which is to hinder and destroy the ministry, preventing it from reaching its destiny.

And do not give the devil an opportunity [to lead you into sin by holding a grudge, or nurturing anger, or harboring resentment, or cultivating bitterness]. **Ephesians 4:27 AMP**

Prophetic snipers God has anointed to cover leaders will receive divine insight and tactics about covering the heart of leaders so they can continue executing the vision God has given them to accomplish. Notice, I did not say to cover the apostle, prophet, pastor etc. specifically, these are anointed positions that have been ordained by God; therefore, when they are operating in these offices they are operating under the anointing of Jesus Christ. However, when they are not under the anointing, they become the man or woman of God. They are also humans with human flaws. It can be very unfair at times when they are unable to be authentic and acknowledge that they hurt as well. **They are not super humans.** Even Jesus had moment of humanity in the Garden of Gethsemane.

And He came out and went, as was His habit, to the Mount of Olives; and the disciples followed Him. [40] When He arrived at the place [called Gethsemane], He said to them, "Pray *continually* that you may not fall into temptation." [41] And He withdrew from them about a stone's throw, and knelt down and prayed, [42] saying, "Father, if You are willing, remove this cup [of divine wrath] from Me; yet not My will, but [always] Yours be done." [43] [d]Now an angel appeared to Him from heaven, strengthening Him. [44] And being in agony [deeply distressed and anguished; almost to the point of death], He prayed more intently; and His [e]sweat became like drops of blood, falling down on the ground. [45] When He rose from prayer, He came to the disciples and found them sleeping from sorrow, [46] **and He said to them, "Why are you sleeping? Get up and pray that you may not fall into temptation." Luke 22:39-46**

83

In verse 46, while Jesus was going through a moment of humanity, his intercessors were sleeping as he was seeking the Lord. The leader's focus should always remain on the vision and seeking the Lord for the next level of obedience to his will. The disciples could not stay awake because of the sorrow they were experiencing, perhaps due to all they had seen Jesus go through while on his way to his assignment (the cross). But notice what Jesus said – **he warned them to pray that they may not fall into temptation.**

When you are covering a major assignment, the appointed prophetic sniper may be prey themselves to the enemy. Right after the above incident, Judas betrayed Jesus. The prophetic sniper must remain in an elevated place of prayer in order to carry the weight of the assignment and the warfare. Remaining in an elevated place also helps the sniper to continue in obedience in order to carry out the vision and assignment by God.

Understanding the Ruler Spirit

We can look at "the spirit of the ruler" from several different perspectives. In a general sense, the ruler may be the leader of a nation, the mayor of a city, the boss at work, the teacher at school, the pastor in a church, or a father of a family. In other words, the ruler is someone in a position of authority. Now there are several ways in which that ruler has spiritual influence over those **under his authority.**

> If a ruler hearken to lies, all his servants are wicked.
> Proverbs 29:12 KJV

The leader is commissioned to rule, which means he is called to exercise his authority and control as governed by God. We will discuss the governing anointing in Chapter 9. If the leader walks in any type of **willful disobedience**, they may fall prey to "the ruler spirit" of this world. The prophetic sniper must continuously pray for purity and sanctification for leaders. Remember, the sniper must target any open place the enemy is attempting to taint and corrupt. This is the place where God has intended to bring him glory.

> Unto the pure all things are pure; but unto them that are defiled and unbelieving is nothing pure, but even their mind and conscience is defiled, 16 They profess that they know God; but in works they deny him, being abominable, and disobedient, and unto every good work reprobate. **Titus 1:15-16**

Prophetic snipers <u>must</u> contend against anything that is not pure. The ultimate goal of the enemy is to strip the purity of God and taint the things and assignments of God. Snipers must remember to pray against **falsehoods, compromise, religion, perversion, every counterfeit entity that attempts to replace the truth.** The enemy will send his agents as angels of light in an attempt to make their abode in the mist of God's work. An effective sniper will immediately spot the enemy and pray exposure to every demonic plot. The sniper may discern demonic activity even while someone may be preaching and prophesying. The sniper will always sense when something is not pure and should begin to ask God to reveal truth – because God discerns the heart through his spirit. Leaders must always remain vigilant to ensure that their assignment remains pure and that they are operating in the Spirit of Truth.

> Howbeit when he, the Spirit of truth, is come, he will guide you into all truth: for he shall not speak of himself; but whatsoever he shall hear, that shall he speak: and he will shew you things to come. He shall glorify me: for he shall receive of mine, and shall shew it unto you. All things that the Father hath are mine: therefore said I, that he shall take of mine, and shall shew it unto you. **John 16:13-15**

Under the Authority of the Ruler

Those under the authority of the ruler may simply model his behavior. If the student observes the teacher or role model acting in a certain way, then he may mimic the teacher and act the exact same way. This is "modeling the behavior" of the authority figure. The little boy often wants to be just like his daddy.

> Walk with the wise and become wise, for a companion of fools suffers harm. **Proverbs 13:20**

> Blessed is the man that walketh not in the counsel of the ungodly, nor standeth in the way of sinners, nor sitteth in the seat of the scornful. **Psalm 1:1**

Those under the authority of the ruler may act a certain way to get or keep the approval and the attention of the person in authority. This may be forced behavior as in the military or voluntary as in business.

> Then the king arose, and tare his garments, and lay on the earth; and all his servants stood by with their clothes rent. And it came to pass, as soon as he had made an end of speaking, that, behold, the king's sons came, and lifted up their voice and wept; and the king also and all his servants wept very sore. **2 Samuel 13:31, 36**

Those submitted under authority may be strongly influenced by an evil spirit in which the authority may carry. This is probably the most dangerous and most unrecognized tactic of the enemy. If a pastor or other church leader has or is influenced by an evil spirit, his congregation or the people under the leader's authority may well be influenced by the same evil spirit – without even recognizing it.

> If a ruler hearken to lies, all his servants are wicked. Proverbs 29:12 KJV

Any God ordained authority over a people is meant to be a channel of God's blessings and an **umbrella of protection** for God's people, because he is the minister of God (**Romans 13:4**). But what if that authority is an evil influence upon the group of people? What if there are "holes" in the umbrella? The prophetic sniper stands in the gap to pray God keeps the connection strong with leaders and the people.

Tactics:

1) **Snipers should pray for God to patch up any "holes" there may be in the umbrella of protection.**

2) **When considering submitting to any authority, the sniper should inquire of the Lord about "the spirit of the ruler".**

> Beloved, believe not every spirit, but try the spirits whether they are of God: because many false prophets are gone out into the world. 1 John 4:1 KJV

Spiritual Discernment

Prophetic intercessors must have a certain level of consecration on their lives in order to obtain a sniper's level of discernment. This enables insight and the ability to pray and legislate spiritual matters. Consecration allows the sniper to effectively "partner" with the Holy Spirit. It is God's spirit that reveals what is transpiring in the spirit realm – both evil and good. God will also reveal his purpose for the assignment that has been entrusted to the leader. Often times, this will come directly from the leader when he casts his vision (what God has given him to accomplish in a set time, set season, or in the earth for kingdom).

Now we have received, not the spirit of the world, but the [Holy] Spirit who is from God, so that we may know and understand the [wonderful] things freely given to us by God. 13 We also speak of these things, not in words taught or supplied by human wisdom, but in those taught by the Spirit, combining and interpreting spiritual thoughts with spiritual words [for those being guided by the Holy Spirit].14 But the natural [unbelieving] man does not accept the things [the teachings and revelations] of the Spirit of God, for they are foolishness [absurd and illogical] to him; and he is incapable of understanding them, because they are spiritually discerned and appreciated, [and he is unqualified to judge spiritual matters]. 15 But the spiritual man [the spiritually mature Christian] judges all things [questions, examines and applies what the Holy Spirit reveals], yet is himself judged by no one [the unbeliever cannot judge and understand the believer's spiritual nature]. 16 For WHO HAS KNOWN THE MIND and PURPOSES OF THE LORD, SO AS TO INSTRUCT HIM? But we have the mind of Christ [to be guided by His thoughts and purposes]. **1 Corinthians 2:12-16**

PROPHETIC ACTIVATION:

Lord, I pray now that you will shift me to another level in my discernment. Help me to see what is transpiring spiritually (what you trust me to see) so I may pray effectively. I ask for your mind and heart so I may know your purpose and plans for covering my leader(s), my church, the region and any assignment you have released to me. I thank you for it now in

In Jesus' Name! Amen.

CHAPTER 9

THE GOVERNMENTAL ANOINTING

There is no authority except from God, and those that exist have been instituted by God. —
Romans 13:1

Jesus answered [Pilate], "You would have no authority over me at all unless it had been given you from above." — **John 19:11**

~

This chapter is very important because a *governmental anointing* in prayer is needed when there is an assignment for a larger territory or a region. Most ministries have actually hindered the region God wants to move in, build something new in, or enlarge simply because there is no strategy in place to execute the agenda of heaven on behalf of God. Leaders and intercessors must move in sync in order to birth out God's will for a particular territory.

Now, this revelation is not for the immature intercessor who may still be in the process of embracing, learning and discovering their gift. This revelation is for **heavy weights**. This intelligence is for the intercessor who has successfully mastered their "specific" process; have mastered a disciplined spiritual life; and have effectively endured as a prophetic sniper. They truly understand the enemy's tactics and are skilled enough spiritually to counteract his attacks. I believe we are in the days where God is ready to pour out his Glory in the earth like never before! Heaven is waiting to release this weight of glory in homes, ministries, regions, and the nation. He is just waiting to hear a sound from the earth! BLOW YOUR TRUMPET! SOUND THE ALARM!

> If my people, which are called by my name, shall humble themselves, and pray, and seek my face, and turn from their wicked ways; then will I hear from heaven, and will forgive their sin, and will heal their land. **2 Chronicles 7:14 KJV**

What is a Governmental Anointing?

The word **government** comes from the Hebrew word *sawraw* which means to prevail or to have power (authority) over as a prince. The Greek word *kurios* means supreme in authority. This means that God is raising up the church to prevail over any powers of darkness on planet earth. We are in a time now where he is already releasing this type of anointing. Likewise, the enemy also has a governmental structure which enables demonic works. Although the enemy is not omnipresent and he cannot rule nations, we must acknowledge that there are demonic systems in place.

Let's take a look at Moses as a type of **governmental** example: he was in a system of bondage erected by Pharaoh and the Egyptians. Moses could have done things his way in order to deliver the Israelites out of Satan's governmental structure, but God released a governmental anointing on Moses at the burning bush. This type of anointing was not intended to deliver a few Israelites but he received a mantle that would deliver an entire nation. This mantle was meant to address the highest office in the land (Pharaoh) which had the entire nation of Israel imprisoned in a demonic system of bondage. God has given your leaders the spiritual authority to contend with governors, representatives, and systems in the region or territory in which they have been assigned to invade, reform or cultivate. Every region needs an apostolic leader to govern God's plan – heaven's agenda on earth.

> I exhort therefore, that, first of all, supplications, prayers, intercessions, and giving of thanks, be made for all men;[2] For kings, and for all that are in authority; that we may lead a quiet and peaceable life in all godliness and honesty.[3] For this is good and acceptable in the sight of God our Saviour;[4] Who will have all men to be saved, and to come unto the knowledge of the truth. **1 Timothy 2:1-4 KJV**

> Let every person be subject to the governing authorities. For there is no authority except from God and those that exist have been instituted by God. **Romans 13:1 ESV**

Here is proof that God has given governmental authority to rule in a region. This type of cultivation not only helps the region, but it pleases God and offers fulfillment to spiritual supporters who have assisted in executing the assignment.

> But seek the welfare of the city where I have sent you into exile and pray to the Lord on its behalf, for in its welfare you will find your welfare. **Jeremiah 29:7 ESV**

A **governmental anointing** will *shake* the systems of the enemy concerning entire families, to religious churches, cities and nations. Entire families and cultures will surrender their lives to Jesus. The church is going to shake the nations! Before Christ comes back, the most powerful institution will be the church; therefore, snipers with a governmental anointing must obtain strategy and instructions from their leader regarding next level in vision and next level in assignments.

When God needed change for a new system of access, the Lord spoke to Moses and commanded him to tell the Levites to bear the Ark of the covenant upon their shoulders. It was because of this reason God struck Uzzah when they were transporting the Ark. Moses did not follow God's instructions completely. In scripture, shoulders symbolize government or a type of authority and power; access. Here, the Levites were ushering a new move or a new "system" of access to God and this new system needed to be carried "upon the shoulders."

The governmental anointing was most apparent on Jesus. The prophet Isaiah prophesied to us in **Isaiah 9:6, For unto us a Child is born, unto us a Son is given; and the government shall be upon his shoulders.** He was the Lamb of God used to usher in an entire system of reconciliation for an entire people back to the Father.

Shoulders also symbolize suffering. Jesus carried the cross on his shoulders all the way to Calvary. Those who are unwilling to go through the "fellowship" of his suffering which is *through* the cross, will not see nor can they carry the POWER of his resurrection. We must be ready to suffer for the sake of the kingdom. Moses was the first of many, Daniel refused to bow to idols and Joseph refused to fall into adultery. Only tested vessels who have remained faithful in the furnace of affliction will move in this type of governmental, *system-shaking*, anointing.

The Burden of the Lord

A burden is something that is typically carried o r a load. A burden can also be a duty or some type of responsibility. Likewise, a burden may be something oppressive or worrisome.

So Moses said to the Lord, "Why have you been so hard on your servant? And why have I not found favor in your sight; that You have laid the burden of all this people on me? **Numbers 11:11KJV**

Here we see that God will place a burden on the leader(s) to accomplish a task he has been anointed for so the leader(s) can execute. Often, there are times where the leader cannot accomplish the task alone. The prophetic intercessor should be moved with compassion to bear this burden along with the leader. **Galatians 6:5, for each one will bear his own load.** The intercessor should hear and intentionally listen to the heart of their leader and they must be open and available to bear the burden of the assignment with the leader. The assignment can be a burden to save souls, build a project for the kingdom, feed the homeless, and etc. Often times, the leader's burden(s) will line up directly with his over-arching vision for the ministry.

There should be compassion and willingness to help decrease the weight of the burden(s). If the intercessor has no compassion to cooperate after a season, then the leader (through wisdom) should seek out another vessel or vessels that are willing. **If the leader does not seek out anointed, competent and appointed help, the burdens may become unbearable.** God instructed Moses to secure able men to help him with the burden of his assignment and to impart his spirit into them.

"The LORD therefore said to Moses, 'Gather for Me seventy men from the elders of Israel, whom you know to be the elders of the people and their officers and bring them to the tent of meeting, and let them take their stand there with you. "Then I will come down and speak with you there, and I will take of the Spirit who is upon you, and will put Him upon them; and they shall bear the burden of the people with you, so that you will not bear it all alone. **Numbers 11:16**

Often times, some intercessors may not be equipped to carry this level of burden due to 4 spirits that will attack:

1) **The spirit of need** – A burden of an assignment *cannot* be effectively built with "needy" people.

2) **The spirit of slumber** – Intercessors must awake out of slumber in order to war and fight for the promise or assignment.

3) **The spirit of not enough** – Not having "enough" to finish the assignment given. Examples: not enough prayer, not enough consecration, not enough wisdom and endurance. etc.

4) **The spirit of self-gain** – The individual is all about themselves and how they are going to benefit. They have underlying motives which can turn into witchcraft. Their heart is **not** to please God, but their heart is to please themselves.

Apostolic Order

God is establishing apostolic order and he is releasing apostolic grace upon leaders with an authorization to use the inherent power of Jesus Christ to fulfill his purpose. **This authority requires TOTAL obedience and complete follow-through for this type of authority to be effective.**

The **governmental anointing** operates properly within this type of order or system. It can be a collaboration of success between the apostle and appointed prophetic intercessor(s). The apostle should appoint governing anointing's over every gate of ministry. The apostles should set order *as it pleases God*.

Apostolic Gates - Governmental Strategy

When Nehemiah was burdened with an assignment from the Lord to rebuild the city of Jerusalem, he went to survey the assignment because he had a passion to be obedient to this task. He completed the work in just 52 Days (**Nehemiah 6:15**). Nehemiah had favor with officials in the land which allowed him to secure the resources he needed to execute this divine assignment. God continued to make every pathway straight for Nehemiah. There were different gates built into the new structure, which I believe is very relevant for the end time. A **governing anointing** is necessary for these key areas – the gates. Here are a few important gates that should be considered when building an effective ministry.

The Fish Gate – This gate refers to the fishers of men. This specific gate requires the governing anointing of someone who is evangelistic and can win souls.

> As Jesus walked beside the Sea of Galilee, he saw Simon and his brother Andrew casting a net into the lake, for they were fishermen. "Come, follow me," Jesus said, "and I will send you out to fish for people." [18] At once they left their nets and followed him. **Mark 1:16-18 NIV**

The Sheep Gate – Here is the gate where sheep were brought into the city to be sacrificed at the altar. The sheep gate represents the lamb of God, whose blood was shed on the cross. This gate requires a governing anointing that can help bring deliverance. The vessel at this gate should also have an anointing to help the sheep walk into their new identity as a Christian. A prophetic intercessor with an anointing of sanctification and deliverance would be ideal at this gate.

The Fountain Gate – This is the gate which reminds us instantly of the words of the Lord to the woman at the well **John 4:14, But**

whoever drinks the water that I give him will never be thirsty again. But the water that I give him will become in him a spring of water [satisfying his thirst for God] welling up [continually flowing, bubbling within him] to eternal life." This is a gate that needs the governing anointing of one who is anointed to cause the rivers of the Lord to flow in a place of worship.

The Water Gate – Water is a symbol of the word of God. The interesting thing about the water gate is that it did not need to be repaired. This was the only part of the wall that was still standing. The word of God will last. Therefore this gate needs the governing anointing of someone who is anointed to teach the word of God with power to help the people of God grow. TEACHERS ARISE!

> Wherein I suffer trouble, as an evil doer, even unto bonds; but the word of God is not bound. **2 Timothy 2:9**

The East Gate – The east gate faced the rising sun and it is considered the gate of hope. It is the gate of anticipation. This gate is needed as a beacon of hope for the people of God. The east gate is a prophetic gate. This gate requires prophetic people and prophets to bring encouragement and prosperity through prophecy. This gate must be restored back to churches that lack hope and progression.

> Surely the Lord GOD will do nothing, but he revealeth his secret unto his servants the prophets. The lion hath roared, who will not fear? the Lord GOD hath spoken, who can but prophesy? **Amos 3:7-8**

The Horse Gate – A horse in scripture is a symbol of warfare or, in this case, the need to do battle against the forces of darkness.

We are not contending against flesh and blood, but against spiritual powers. This gate needs the governing anointing of a prophetic sniper who can war against the enemy and declare the promises of God through prayer.

> Fight the good fight of faith, lay hold on eternal life, whereunto thou art also called, and hast professed a good profession before many witnesses. **1 Timothy 6:12**

The Dung Gate – Here is where they carried the waste from the city. All of the rubbish and filth of the city was taken out through the dung gate. Apostolic people should be positioned at the gate. One that can declare holiness and right living. An apostolic anointing helps to clean up the "mess" and bring order. **This vessel must have boldness!**

> For God hath not called us unto uncleanness, but unto holiness. **1 Thessalonians 4:7**

> Make every effort to live in peace with everyone and to be holy; without holiness no one will see the Lord. **Hebrews 12:14**

The goal for *Prophetic Snipers, Volume 1* was to provide foundational insight and strategy about what God is doing now in the area of intercession and in the lives of modern-day intercessors. **You have successfully completed basic camp.** This is just the beginning and I hope you will continue on this Sniper journey of deeper insight and more strategy. We will resume this journey in *Prophetic Snipers, Volume 2.*

Gone are the days of old school intercession...**welcome to next level intercession and welcome to the new breed!**

APOSTOLIC PRAYER:

Lord, I thank you now for the submission to apostolic authority, I thank you for choosing me to help assist and help carry the burden of the assignment that you have given to my leaders. I thank you Lord that I am graced for this task with boldness, strength and power. I give up the ground to buck against the order and my assignment to assist. I am a mature sniper and I will endure through to the end.

Lord, I thank you for this end time, governmental anointing that will attract apostolic intercessors to accomplish your will in the region in which you have assigned to my church leaders.

I pray a travailing anointing to engulf my life to help birth out a move of God for my region. This anointing will cause a drawing by your spirit for salvation, deliverance and healing as in 2 Chronicles 7:14. If my people, which are called by my name, shall humble themselves, and pray, and seek my face, and turn from their wicked ways; then will I hear from heaven, and will forgive their sin, and will heal their land.

I thank you now that this governmental anointing will shift, cities, and nations while covering our president, vice president, city officials and governors.

In Jesus' Name! Amen.

- **NOTES** -

ABOUT THE AUTHOR

Teri Jones has been spiritually trained in the art of strategic warfare prayer and is a skilled prophetic intercessor with sharpshooter accuracy. She is a spiritual marksman, validated as a governmental prophet with an apostolic-prophetic anointing. She has a burning desire to see people walking unbound and purposely in their destinies.

Teri Jones resides in Atlanta, GA and is married to the love of her life, Berrell Jones.

———

For more information about Teri Jones, Prophetic Snipers, bookings, on-site training sessions, and workshops, go to:

www.terijonesministries.com

Made in the USA
Columbia, SC
24 November 2024

47443368R00063